CAST OUT

Queen

By

Kaye Hohst

Cast Out Queen

Cast Out Queen by Kaye Hohst

Illustration by Veronica Peterson

Published by CreateSpace Independent Publishing Platform
www.createspace.com

Copyright © 2016 by Kaye Hohst
All rights reserved.
ISBN: 0692548688
ISBN-13: 978-0692548684

The content in this book is based on true events. Names and some events have been altered to protect the identity of those involved.

Cast Out Queen

Acknowledgements

I would like to thank my Lord and Savior Jesus Christ, whom all things are possible. It is truly amazing how He takes difficult circumstances and creates miracles. He certainly did this in my life.

I also could not have completed this without my husband's support. He has always believed in me and encouraged me to use the gifts and talents God has graciously given. I am forever grateful to you.

Thank you to my Mother, who planted the seed that I had a gift of writing. She obediently passed along the message God had given to her concerning my purpose in His Kingdom. Thank you, Mom.

Thank you to my daughter Kayla for being the first to read the draft of this story and encouraging me to get it published. You boosted my self-esteem and gave me hope to continue.

Thank you to my son, Michael for listening to my endless barrages of hopes and dreams. He always has an encouraging word and provided great advice in many areas. What a blessing you've been in my life.

Lastly, I want to express my appreciation to my daughter, Veronica. She was my go to concerning my walk with God. She listened and spoke with discernment and showed me that if we listen close, we can hear God's will for our lives.

Thank you all for your support.

TABLE OF CONTENTS

Shock	1
Monster	9
Violation	15
The Move	24
First Day	31
Saved	38
Truth	44
Rescue	52
Blossom	61
The Dance	69
Freedom	78
Slave Day	85
Sleep Over	93
Accident	101
Redemption	112
Author's Notes	124
Salvation	129

SHOCK

Desiree searched the dial on the stereo she'd just gotten for Christmas. She stopped when there was a familiar ballad and immersed herself into each word. Concentrating harder, she forced her fears and shame into hiding. As her eyes grew heavy, she began to dream of life without misery and terror. Startled, Desiree heard shouting. "Desi! Meagan! Come quick girls! I have something exciting to tell you!"

Everyone used the shortened version of Desiree and she preferred it as well. She could hear in her mother's voice that it was important, which helped to pry herself away from her favorite pillow. As she made her way to the stairs, Desi sister Meagan approached at the same time.

"Go ahead, Meagan." Desi grumbled.

Without hesitation, Meagan darted down the stairs. They found their mother in the kitchen.

"Well, don't keep us in suspense, Mom." Meagan pushed.

"Yeah, what is it?" Desi agreed.

"Let's see," she teased. "I can't seem to remember."

"Mom!" they both shouted.

Cast Out Queen   K. Hohst

"Okay! Okay! We bought a house just three houses down from Grandma and Grandpa!"

Desi lost all expression. *What is she saying?* She thought. *We're moving? No! This can't be!*

"We're moving in three weeks, if all goes as planned." her mother added.

As the shock of the news sank in, Desi's usual submissive behavior instantly turned.

"I'm not going and you can't make me!" Desi exploded.

"Desiree Sue Johnson. I see you are upset but…" She stopped, realizing what her daughter must be feeling and continued with a softer tone. "Honey, this move will be good for us. Your Grandma and Grandpa will be just down the street."

Desi ached to scream. *Yeah,* she thought. *I know why you want to live near Grandma and Grandpa. Dad won't try to hurt you if they're just down the street! And how is that my fault? Why should my life change because you married him?*

She kept this to herself, although she probably could have gotten away with it because she rarely stood up for herself. Not to mention this was devastating news and her mother new it.

"Desi, you'll like it there. You won't have as much mowing to do." she tried again.

Everyone counted on Desi to do the yard. She loved to be outdoors and barefoot. "She's not afraid of a little dirt!" they would say. While Desi didn't mind this, her true desire was to be more like her older sister. Meagan meant the world to Desi. Not only was she thin with beautiful blonde hair and blue eyes, she was also confident and delicate in her smaller frame. She was everything Desi wasn't and more. Her room was always meticulous, she was very popular, and she seemed to be good at anything she tried. Meagan was two years older and it seemed that Desi was always a step behind in everything.

Desi took a moment to absorb her mother's words and realized that she was getting nowhere. Defeated, she retreated to her room but left her mother with a strong message as she slammed the door.

Desi's emotions swelled until she couldn't hold them any longer. As the tears came, the fears and anxieties came along with them. *What am I going to do without my best friend, Julie? She is the only friend that I managed to make and that was just plain luck. No one will accept me.* She stared at the mirror, horrified at what she had become.

Cast Out Queen   K. Hohst

At the mere age of 13, her weight had climbed to 150 pounds. She was also forced to wear glasses due to ongoing headaches. To top it off, puberty brought with it a lovely skin condition to accent her freckles and blue eyes. Unable to bear the sight of her unruly brown hair, Desi buried her face into the nearest pillow and sobbed.

Dear God! Are you there? How can I face another school and more rejection? It was hard enough at this one! I've never fit in! Do you think the next school is going to be any different?

Desi often turned to God. He was the only one she could truly be honest with. At the age of five, her Aunt Isabelle took on the role of spiritual leadership for her and Meagan by faithfully picking them up every Sunday morning for church. Afterwards, she would take them to lunch at the local Mexican restaurant or a meal prepared at her place. Desi clung to God from the first moment.

Desi wept until she heard a gentle knock at the door.

"Desi," Meagan spoke.

She snapped at her sister to go away. She felt repulsive enough without having to look at her perfect sister.

"Desi, open up," she tried again. "Let me help you."

"You can't help me! No one can!"

"Yes, I can. At least let me try."

Reluctantly, Desi drug herself from the bed and opened the door.

"How are you holding up?"

"How do you think?" Desi flopped on the bed.

"You were pretty brave out there with Mom. If that were me... Well, you know what would've happened."

"That's because you argue with her all the time,"

"Maybe, but moving won't be that bad you know."

"Easy for you to say."

"I'm scared too and I have friends here that I don't want to leave."

"You'll never know what it is like to be me okay?"

Desi turned to face the wall so her sister wouldn't see the tears that were about to stream down her face. Knowing this, Meagan turned to what had always worked with Desi in the past.

"Desi…I have a st-o-o-ry," she enticed.

Meagan had this uncanny ability to bring the best and the worst out of Desi. Not many people had the capability of making Desi truly laugh, but she had a way of telling a story with emotional perfection.

Desi sniffled.

"Come on, it's a good one."

Desi grumbled.

"Well, do you want to hear it or not?"

"Fine, tell me."

"Do you remember when my friend Denise from church came and spent the night?"

"Yeah, I guess."

"I wasn't going to tell anyone because she begged me not to, but in this case I think she wouldn't mind."

"What? Tell me what?" Desi became more anxious.

"You know how easy it is to get her to laugh, right?"

"Yeah and…?"

Cast Out Queen — K. Hohst

"Well, this time Denise and I were talking about my friend that I was in the play with last spring. I was telling her that in the play my friend had to wear a costume with sparkling purple fringes along her arms because she was a butterfly. Unfortunately for her, in the most crucial point of the play, her wings fell off and she had to hide behind one of the props until the song was over."

Desi began to giggle.

"Anyway, Denise and I were both laughing hysterically, and you won't believe what happened!

"What? Tell me!" Desi agonized.

"Well," Meagan giggled. "Denise laughed so hard that she wet her pants!"

Both Meagan and Desi began to laugh.

"That wasn't the half of it! She didn't have an extra pair of underwear so we had to dry them with the hairdryer.

And then..." Meagan was barely able to speak. "She was drying her underwear and she... she... burned a hole clear through them!"

This time the tears were not of despair or uncertainty, but of sheer bliss. Both the girls hit the floor.

When Desi could finally catch her breath, she asked, "What happened after that?"

"Well, let's just say that I'm missing a pair of underwear now." Meagan giggled and they both broke into laughter again.

"Everything is going to be okay, Desi. Trust me." Meagan assured.

"Maybe," Desi lied.

"I know! Let's do a make-over on you!" Meagan announced. "We'll have you looking fabulous for your new classmates! What do you think?"

"I suppose I wouldn't mind a new look," Desi agreed.

Both were having a great time with make-up, curlers, and clothes. That is, until Dad came home.

MONSTER

"GIRLS!" he bellowed, "Where is my towel?

Instantly, Meagan and Desi began to tremble.

"He's home," Desi shook.

"Calm down, Desi. I'll go this time."

Desi breathed a sigh of relief as her sister rushed down the stairs to get him a towel to dry his hands.

Unbelievable, Desi thought. *Who does he think we are? I swear he only wanted children to complete his dictatorship. Every day was the same thing. Girls, where is my towel. Girls, get my cigarettes. Girls, take my boots off. Get me a Pepsi. Make me some popcorn. Blah! Blah! Blah! I hate him! I wish Mom would just divorce him and get it over with!*

Desi hoped and prayed each day for this, but she knew better. Her parents were raised Amish and it was forbidden to divorce for any reason. Not only that, Desi's mother knew what would happen if she tried to leave him again. Every incident grew more violent and each day that passed made it harder for her mother to face the world alone with two daughters and no prospects of work.

Desi was much like her Mother. She had some of the same physical attributes; however, it was personality that built the bond between them. Both were passive in nature and would go out of their way to help anyone in need. Perhaps, helping others was a coping mechanism for both, feeling a sense of purpose and a genuine concern that lifted their spirits.

Desi's Father on the other hand, was foreign to her in every way. He was aggressive, loud, self-centered, demanding, and "making his million" was the focal point of his life. Perfectionism was quite the understatement and those around him were given extremely high expectations that often failed. Rage often followed. He was extremely impatient with Desi's mother and it was terrifying to watch her anxiously try to meet his needs. There were moments that he attempted to bring joy to the family; however, it was always by his own agenda and mostly Desi, Megan and their Mother fictitiously played the part.

While Dad was home, life for Desi consisted of high intensity fear, walking on eggshells, and avoidance at all costs. Her Father was an early riser in the mornings but then always took a nap in the afternoons. It was during these times that everyone was subject to silence. There was an incident when Desi was four years old and she'd fallen down the wooden stairs. Desi, of course was crying in pain. Again, her Father was taking a nap and Megan's mother did her best to hush Desi's crying. Trying not to wake Dad took precedence over anyone or anything.

Meagan often took the role of soothing Desi's fears either through humor or affection. Although Megan often irritated and instigated arguments, she was also the first to protect her little sister. Both loved to climb the trees in the front yard and would spend hours sitting on one of the branches wishing God would rescue them from their Father.

Desi couldn't help but hear her father shouting downstairs as he chastised her sister for having to wait for a towel after he washed his hands from another day out in the fields.

The Johnson's lived on a large farm with a two-story white farm house, an elaborate shop with multiple barns, and topped with newly built silos. The silos were his most recent accomplishment, which of course would be the next subject for him to boast about at a family get together or even to a perfect stranger for that matter.

Are you there, God? Spare us this agony! Desi pleaded. *Make it stop. Make him go away! Anything, Lord. Just do something! Please!*

Meagan retreated upstairs as soon as the opportunity was given. Desi watched her sister closely trying to read her expression to see how bad it was this time.

"Thanks, Meagan."

"It's all right, Desi. Someday he won't have control over us anymore and we won't have to live like this. So, don't you worry about it, okay?"

Desi could sense the fear in Meagan's voice but she pretended that she believed her.

"Komm essen!" their mother called.

This was often spoken when it was time for dinner. Though the family didn't dress or act Amish anymore, they still tried to get them to learn the Amish language. They had left the Amish church when Desi was only a year old and this made them the target of jokes and teasing when it was time to get together with their Dad's side of the family. By being the only one in the family to convert at the time, made it easy for the entire clan to consider them the black sheep.

"Come eat!" their mother called again.

Desi and Meagan just looked at each other, both afraid to face the monster. Finally, they knew they had to go before their dad would get involved.

Tension was in the air as they sat eating supper. No one dared say anything. Most of the time they were left to guess what it was that put him in a mood. Was it work or was it something that their mother had done? No one knew for sure, but one thing was certain, never under any circumstances try to defend yourself.

The only sound that could be heard throughout dinner was the tapping of forks and an occasional sip of water. Manners were of great importance at the table, and if

you were caught talking with your mouth full or even causing an accidental spill, you were sure to be yelled at.
Most of the time their mother would try to console the girls, but there were times when she knew when to keep her mouth shut.

"Where is the *real* butter?" he asked. "You know I don't like that fake stuff!"

"We ran out of it, and I haven't made it to the store yet to get some."

"Girls, go upstairs. Dinner is over," he commanded.

They immediately left the table and went upstairs. The girls sat and waited, wondering how bad it would turn out this time. They could hear the shouting from their dad and the trembling of their mother's voice. The girls remained quiet, fearing his anger would turn on them. They didn't hear him hitting her though the fear was just as real as if he were. Soon, the door slammed and all was quiet. The girls knew that it was safe to go downstairs.

Without being told, they began doing the dishes. The abuse was always apparent but never discussed. They would just go on as if nothing happened and try to be as nice and quiet as possible.

The rest of the evening was spent hoping and praying that he wouldn't return or at the very least until they were fast asleep.

The next morning was as if nothing had ever happened. At breakfast, he was his obnoxious self again by teasing Desi about her weight and striking up awkward conversation. It was as if he was trying to make up for the damage done the previous night.

"So, Desi. How many pancakes can you eat today?" he laughed.

Playing along Desi spoke, "Oh, probably six or seven," she said with a fake chuckle.

"And how are you this morning, Meagan?" he patronized.

"Just great Dad," she managed to mutter.

"Well, that is just fantastic!"

It was bittersweet getting ready for the bus. Desi could escape her father, but it was the last day of school, and that meant it would soon be time to move to their new home. Desi had accepted the move by this time. Her fears and anxieties about the move still remained, but would be well hidden.

VIOLATION

To celebrate the last day of school, Desi planned to spend the night with Skyler, a friend who lived down the road. Since Desi lived on a farm, she decided to ride her mini bike that she'd gotten for Christmas to the sleep over. Skyler was older than Desi and she really was unsure of why she wouldn't want to hang out with Meagan instead. They were certainly more compatible since both were popular, beautiful, and had plenty of boyfriends they could share stories about. Still, Desi was flattered to have been asked over to her house.

When Desi arrived, Skyler's mother opened the door and kindly welcomed her inside. Her Dad and brother were sitting in the living room watching football. Desi didn't know much about Skyler's brother, other than he was a senior in High School and they rode the same bus to school. He was tall and thin with brown curly hair. He nodded at Desi as she walked by. Desi was too intimidated to speak so she just smiled back.

Their home was also a two story farmhouse but was more cluttered. Desi didn't mind, however, and felt comfortable in her surroundings. She'd never been inside their house. Up until now, Desi had only been in their swimming pool or in the yard playing.

"Hi Desi!" Skyler warmly smiled.

"Hey." Desi shyly replied.

"What do you want to do tonight?" Skyler asked.

"I don't know. What do you want to do?"

Desi rarely expressed her own interests and was more comfortable putting other people's preferences first.

Skyler thought for a moment then asked, "Do you want to watch a movie in my room? We could get pizza and make popcorn if you want."

"Sounds good to me. What movies do you have?

"I'll show you once we get upstairs. Do you want to watch something scary or funny?"

"Either one is fine." Desi offered.

"You're easy to please." she added.

"Yeah, yeah." Desi giggled.

After the girls had picked out a movie and, they gathered all the pillows they could find and settled in with pizza and popcorn. Desi finally felt more as ease and was really enjoying the sleep over. After watching two movies, Skyler suggested they call it a night. Her bedroom had two twin beds.

"I'm exhausted," Skyler exclaimed.

"Me too," Desi agreed.

"Which bed do you want to sleep in?" Skyler asked.

"It doesn't matter to me."

"Well, you take the one next to the wall then."

"That's fine."

Both changed into their pajamas then laughed and talked for a while before drifting off to sleep.

It was still dark outside when Desi suddenly awoke. She was disoriented and tried to remember where she was. When she determined that she was at Skyler's house, she realized that something was terribly wrong. Lying on her back, she felt something in between her legs. Desi froze. Her mind began to race trying to figure out who or what was invading her. As disturbing as it was, she first thought maybe it was Skyler but soon thought better of it. Desi thoughts then turned to her friend's brother Jack. Surely not, she cringed. She just laid there frozen with fear and disgust while this cruel person used their mouth and tongue to assault her. It was pitch black in the room so she was unable to decipher anything at that point.

Oh God, Desi thought. What do I do? Why can't I move or do something to make it stop? I feel sick to my stomach. How long will this last? Oh God! Make it stop! Please!

Suddenly, he stopped and Desi heard a voice.

"Desi." he whispered.

Desi didn't respond as she confirmed it was Skyler's brother.

"Desi." he tried again.

She finally gave in.

"What?" her voice shook.

"Can I get in bed with you?" he responded.

Desi emphatically stated, "NO!"

To Desi's surprise, he immediately turned and went across the hall to his room, although she was terrified that he would return. She didn't know what to do. She realized he'd removed her underwear and she struggled to find them in the dark. She finally found them under the covers and not caring if they were inside out or not, Desi put them back on. Her stomach continued to churn and she felt as if the pizza and popcorn she'd eaten was going to come back up.

Desi was too terrified to wake Skyler so she just laid there watching the door, hoping he would not return. Unfortunately, he did. She heard his door open and tip toe across the hall. Just as he began to enter the bedroom again,

Desi tried to shout and whisper at the same time for him to go away. He again retreated.

This time Desi could no longer hold in her feelings as she sat up began to sob. Skyler began to stir as she heard Desi's crying. She immediately was at Desi's side.

Concerned, Skyler asked, "What is wrong, Desi?"

Sniffling, Desi replied "Your brother asked if he could get into bed with me."

Skyler was shocked and asked, "Are you sure you weren't dreaming?"

"No, it wasn't a dream." Desi defended. She wanted to tell Skyler what he had done to her but she didn't know what it was called and she certainly couldn't form the words to even describe it.

Skyler immediately went and told her parents. She returned and stated they would deal with it in the morning. For now, they needed to go back to sleep. Desi was horrified that she was going to have to stay there. She laid there for what seemed like forever just staring at the door in terror. Finally, fatigue from crying took over and she fell asleep.

As soon as Desi awoke the next morning, she grabbed her things as quickly as possible. No one else was up yet and she ran out the door. Desi was grateful that the mini bike started up right away so she could escape without notice. The ride home was cold and terrifying. Her hands were shaking so violently that she was barely able to steer the bike. All she could think about was getting to the safety of her own home. She longed for her warm bed and favorite pillow. Desi recognized the irony of how home was normally a source of fear, yet now was a source of safety.

When she arrived home, she wanted to run into her mother's arms but again had no words to describe what had happened. Instead, she crawled into bed and hid under the covers. Desi was mindful to lay on her side, as she'd awoken to the horror while lying on her back. She wondered how something so awful could have happened to her and turned to the One who she could always count on.

Father, I'm afraid. How could he do this to me? It was so awful, Lord. Why? Why me? I don't think Skyler believed me or her parents for that matter. I don't think anyone will. How will I survive this? Are you there God? Can you hear me? What should I do? Will you protect me? I'm so scared.

Desi had so many questions and no answers for any of them. Confusion and fear gripped her and she continued to pray until she drifted to sleep.

A few hours later, her mother called for her to wake up. Meagan had heard Desi come in earlier and told her mother that she was sleeping. Desi didn't want to move from the security of her room but knew she would have to.

She got dressed and brushed her teeth. Then ate her breakfast in silence.

"Why are you home so early from Skyler's, Desi?" her mother asked.

"I woke up before anyone else so I decided to leave."

Desi was thankful that she didn't have to actually tell a lie to her mother.

Megan noticed her sister's mood and immediately could sense there was something terribly wrong. After breakfast, Megan asked Desi to come to her room and she closed the door.

"What is the matter, Desi?" Megan probed.

Desi was silent.

"Did something happen at Skyler's?" she tried again.

Desi began to cry.

Megan urgently asked again, "What happened, Desi? You have to tell me!"

Desi finally broke her silence and told Megan everything except for what he'd done to her physically.

Furious, Meagan shouted, "That is horrible, Desi! I'm so sorry! I'm going to go tell Mom."

Megan left the room and Desi ached to tell her sister the truth but she just couldn't. It was too devastating and embarrassing. Desi went back to her room and soon Megan returned.

"I told Mom."

"What did she say?" Desi asked.

"She wasn't very happy and said she would take care of it. Whatever that means."

"Was she mad at me?"

"Not at all!" Megan assured.

"Is she going to tell Dad?"

"I don't know, Desi."

"How do you think he will react to it if she does?"

"I wouldn't want to be Jack if Dad finds out. That's for sure. Are you going to be alright, Desi? Is there anything you need?"

Desi lied. "I'm fine. I just want to forget it ever happened and I never want to see him again."

"We ride the same bus as he does so that isn't possible, Desi."

"I know." Desi agreed.

"It's just a few more weeks and then we are moving. I suppose that is one good thing about moving away. You will never have to see him after that."

Relieved, Desi smiled. "Yeah, that's just fine with me. The sooner. The better."

"I'm really sorry this happened to you, Desi."

Desi wanted to tell Megan exactly how she felt and what he'd done to her but there just seemed no way of saying it. She was even unable to tell her best friend at school. It was just to nauseating to speak the words. So, she accepted that it would have to remain a secret between her and God.

THE MOVE

For the next few weeks, the bus ride was awkward and terrifying for Desi. When Jack would walk past, she would just look down or pretend like she was looking out the window or reading a book. Meagan mentioned to Desi that Jack received a good beating from his parents for his behavior but that was of little comfort. Strangely, Desi's parents never said a word to her about the incident and acted as if it had never happened. Desi was fine with never speaking a word of it again and was relieved when it was never mentioned. The end of the school year had finally arrived and for the first time Desi was excited about the move.

With everything packed up and loaded, the time had come for Desi to say goodbye to the old two-story farmhouse and say hello to a one-story ranch. As they pulled out of the driveway, Desi turned to watch, until the place she called home had faded away.

Many thoughts plagued her mind. She wondered what was in store for her in her new life. Would she be shunned in the new school? Would this mend the troubles that clung to her parent's marriage? Would she be able to get past the incident at the neighbor's?

For a moment, Desi allowed herself to dream the impossible. *Perhaps,* she thought. *I'll lose weight, get contacts, and clear up my face. Yeah, and then maybe I'll be the most beautiful girl in school and I'll have a popular boyfriend!*

She stopped, as reality clobbered her over the head. *It would take a miracle from God to pull that one off,* she thought.

When they arrived at the new house, Desi noticed right away how close the neighbor's houses were to theirs. She found comfort knowing there were others nearby. She also noticed a smaller front yard but a larger back yard that led to the creek. She wondered if she could find solace by the creek bank during times of struggles. There were no trees in the back yard, which would make the mowing much easier. It was just a large stretch of beautiful green grass. It made Desi smile.

Inside, Desi noticed the large mirrors that lined one of the walls. She tried not to focus on her reflection. She quickly turned her attention to the sliding glass doors in the kitchen that highlighted the back-yard view. Desi couldn't deny the fact that she was anxious to see her room. Desi's mother tried to entice her by telling her to pick the room of her choice. Desi tried not to show her excitement, as she didn't want her mother to know she was enjoying the move so far.

"I want this one," Meagan quickly decided.

It must be the biggest one. Desi thought.

Sure enough, Meagan had chosen the larger of the two rooms. Desi covered her disappointment by rationalizing that she won't have as much to clean. She often gave in under the assumption that she should always have second best and in some strange way, even if she had gotten the larger room, she would only have felt guilty and given it to her sister anyway.

Desi stood imagining how her things would look in her new room, when she heard a voice that, in an instant, sent chills down her spine.

"Well, what do you think of your new room?"

Trembling, Desi tried to answer enthusiastically. "It's great, Dad."

"Oh yeah?" his voice intensified. "I thought you'd like it."

There was an awkward silence, and then he went on unpacking.

Desi wondered how it almost seemed as if he was sincerely being nice, yet his mere presence exuded dominance and intimidation.

She focused again on her room and thought, *why would Dad think this room is so great anyway? Now I only have one window instead of four and my room is half the size! It has never been about my happiness so why should it start now? I suppose at night; however, it might not be as scary with only having one window.*

Since the sleep over, nighttime was terrifying. So much so that she couldn't lay in any position except on her side and most of the time covering herself completely with the blankets. She spoke to God many nights until she would finally fall asleep.

The rest of the house was very small compared to the farmhouse, but Desi was happy to have a bathroom just across the hall. The living room was a nice size, but there was no longer a dining room. It was rarely used anyway, Desi decided. She also thought about the smells of the farm that she'd taken for granted, which included the cows, pigs, and the smell of fresh harvested corn in the fields adjacent to them. Desi would certainly miss the long gravel lanes that she could explore with the mini bike and wondered when or if it would ever get used again. Desi focused on decorating her room and tried to silence the ache in her heart.

After a few days, when everything had settled in a bit, things seemed to return to normal routines. Dinner was ready and on the table at 5:30 sharp. That meant it was time for someone to wake dad up from his nap.

"You do it this time, Meagan," Desi begged.

"What are you afraid of? You are the little angel that does no wrong." Meagan exclaimed.

"Fine, I'll do it then!" Desi shouted.

Desi tiptoed all the way down the hall until she faced the doorway. She stood there for a few minutes before she gathered up enough courage to open the door.

"Dad," she barely whispered. "Dad," she tried again.

"Hmm," he mumbled.

"It's time for dinner," her voice shook.

"Okay," he gruffly answered.

That's all she needed to hear and not a second later she was running down the hallway.

Everyone was seated and ready to eat when he finally came straggling to the table. Each one was praying that he was in a good mood. Unfortunately, that would not be the case.

He began by demanding, "Get me my cigarettes!"

With no hesitation, Meagan jumped up and tried as quickly as possible to meet his demand. She set them down next to him and not so much as a thank you followed. They began to eat and it was clear that there was no room for error.

I know he is going to do it. Desi fretted to herself. *He's going to find something to yell at Mom about.*

"Why weren't my clean pants in the drawer this morning?" he complained.

"I didn't have a chance to put them away yesterday," (Knowing full well that it was Desi and Meagan's job to do that)

At this point, the girls were abruptly excused from the table and sent to their rooms.

Desi turned on her stereo in the hopes of tuning out the terrifying sound of her dad's abuse and all the while praying it wouldn't be physical this time. Desi recalled what she'd said about her mother wanting to be close to her parents.

She now admitted to herself that she was glad to be just down the street from the safety of her Grandma and Grandpa.

How could I have blamed her for wanting to move here? Please God. Give her the strength to get through this night! I know you don't approve of divorce, but please God, let her go! One of these days he'll go too far. Please God! Help her!

She continued to pray until she finally fell asleep.

The next morning, Desi didn't leave her room until she was certain that he had left for work. As soon as she was sure, she ran to her mother to see how she was. Luckily, this time there wasn't anything visible though she did seem distraught and shaken.

"Are you okay, Mom?"

"I'm fine, Desi. Thank you."

Desi couldn't work up the courage to tell her mother what she thought of him or what she'd prayed the night before and so, she just sat there with her. After quite some time, her mother must have realized how Desi was feeling and immediately concentrated on making up for her misery.

"Hey! School starts in a few weeks so let's go get you some new clothes! What do you say?"

Desi hesitated. She wanted to be excited for her mother's sake; however, she suddenly had this sick feeling in her stomach at the mere thought of starting a new school. She pulled herself together and finally spoke.

"Okay, Mom, let's go shopping."

Desi temporarily repressed her feelings so her mother wouldn't suspect the truth. Still, underneath, were the layers of anguish, despair and utter fear. Soon, she would have to face each one of these.

FIRST DAY

The first day of school had finally arrived, and Desi tried to muster as much courage as possible.

"Desi!" her mother called. "Desi, get up!" she shouted again.

"I'm up. I'm up," she moaned.

"You don't want to be late for your first day do you?"

Yes. I do, she thought to herself slowly climbing out of bed.

Everyone sat down to breakfast, and it was soon apparent that Dad was in a good mood this time and with his loud voice, he targeted Desi.

"So, it's your first day of school! Are you nervous?"

"A little," Desi answered as she reached for more bacon.

"You sure do like to eat, don't ya?" he blurted.

Desi looked to her mother for refuge and instinctively she defended her.

"She will need to eat enough to last until lunchtime."

He had always made numerous comments about Desi's weight. He would ask, "How much do you weigh now, Desi?" Or he'd say, "Give Desi the biggest baked potato. She'll eat it all." It seemed as if Desi's weight was the only thing that he could connect to.

After the girls were both ready for school, they walked to the end of the driveway to wait for the bus. Desi's stomach was in knots as she stood there torturing herself with thoughts of everyone teasing her and calling her names.

As the bus pulled up, Desi's knees began to shake. The size of the yellow beast seemed to have magnified a few times over since the year before. At least she wouldn't have to see Jack anymore.

She followed Meagan onto the bus and searched for somewhere to sit. It was very full and getting a seat wasn't easy for her. Someone had moved over to let Meagan sit down almost immediately. As Desi walked further down the aisle, she could hear some of the other children snicker and laugh. No one would let her sit down until the bus driver called to one of the children to move over. Meagan glanced back at Desi with a sympathetic look, as if she were letting her know that she was watching out for her.

The remainder of the bus ride seemed to last a lifetime. Starting the first day with humiliation wasn't at all what she had in mind and uncertain of what was ahead, she silently prayed that it would only get better. After a small prayer, she began looking around at the people in her surroundings.

The girl sitting next to her was busy talking to friends and the boys on the other side of the isle were teasing the girls behind them. Diagonally, she noticed a boy who briefly looked at her with a kind and sincere face. He had blond hair and was almost lanky in stature. He turned away after smiling at her and Desi was left wondering who he was and why he seemed so kind to her when everyone else was so rude. Desi managed a small smile as she pondered the small gesture.

After a few wrong turns and aimlessly wondering the hallways, Desi finally located her homeroom. As she walked in she noticed someone that she had gone to Bible School with over the summer.

Oh! Thank you, Lord! Desi thought to herself. *Someone I know!*

"Hello." the teacher pleasantly focused on Desi. "I'm Mrs. Williams. You must be a new student because I don't remember seeing you before."

Desi just smiled trying to hide any sign of terror on her face.

"You may choose your own seat today until I assign you a seat permanently." she added.

With that, Desi slowly looked around the room for an empty seat. She found one next to the familiar face she had seen previously and sat down.

"Hello, Desi."

"Hey, Jena I didn't know that you went to this school."

"Yeah, it's not too bad here. Do you want to sit together at lunch?"

Delighted, Desi answered, "That would be great! Thanks!"

For a moment, Desi could relax a bit and concentrate on something other than rejection or fear. That is, until the bell rang. Desi noticed two girls confidently strolling in the door. Both girls were tall, thin, and wore matching leather jackets. Although, Desi couldn't see what the jackets said on the back, she imagined something along the lines of a skull and cross bones. As they walked towards Desi's row, they noticed the new face in the crowd almost immediately.

"Who's the ugly geek?"

The other girl joined in, "Don't you mean crater face?"

"Oh yeah, that's what I meant."

Both obnoxiously laughed.

Suddenly, any hope Desi had was crushed in a matter of seconds. She was completely humiliated. Mrs. Williams tried unsuccessfully to quiet the girls.

"Now, Lisa and Jackie settle down," she said.

For the remainder of homeroom, the girls concentrated their efforts on how miserable they could make Desi. Not a single jab was missed. Everything from hefty hips to pimple princess was aimed at Desi, and all she could do was sit there and swallow each painful word.

Finally, homeroom was over and Desi's only thought was to escape the ruthlessness by hiding in the bathroom stall. She tried her best to cry without bringing any other attention to herself and after the bell rang, she realized that she'd have to clear up and find a way to gather the courage to go to the next class. Her primary thought was whether the bullies were going to be in any of her other classes.

When Desi finally made it to first period, the teacher abruptly stopped his lesson and welcomed Desi.

"Did you get lost?" he asked.

"Yes." Desi lied.

"Well, come on in and find a seat." he pleasantly replied.

She looked around the room for the girls who tormented her. Luckily, they were nowhere to be found. Instead, she noticed the boy on the bus who had smiled at her. She was grateful. Desi took a seat in the back and spent the entire period agonizing over what the bullies would do to her next.

Lunchtime had finally arrived without any further signs of the girls and so she immediately sought out Jena for comfort from the cold institution. Neither one spoke about what had happened and each pretended nothing was wrong.

Desi admired Jena's short straight blonde hair. It perfectly suited her care free disposition. Desi also took notice of Jena's clear smooth skin and wished she had the same. Her clothes were not too plain but not flashy either. Desi really appreciated Jena's friendship.

Soon, the bullies had made their way into the lunchroom, and Desi prayed that they wouldn't notice her. Unfortunately, they walked right past her and together shouted, "FAT FREEK!"

The entire lunchroom fell silent and then at once was filled with laughter. Jena and Desi just looked at one another and could only feel embarrassment. Jena played it off cool by telling Desi that they were jerks and that nobody liked them anyway.

The rest of the day was pretty much the same. Anytime, the girls saw Desi, they had something to say about and to her. Only one good thing came of the day for Desi; she had no other classes with them except for homeroom and lunch.

When Desi finally reached the safety of home, she tried to rush to her room before her mother could ask how her day was at school. Realistically, this wouldn't be possible.

"How was your day, Desi?"

It took everything she had to pretend as if nothing had happened. Somehow, she convinced her of just that.

"It was fine, Mom. I saw Jena there and we hung out together."

At least she wouldn't have to lie to her mother.

"That's wonderful! Desi! See, I told you things would turn out just fine."

Desi indulged her mother as she continued to express her excitement. But, as soon as she was able, she retreated to her room, not giving anyone else the chance to interrogate her. She spent the rest of the evening wondering how she would go on, and how to trust God.

SAVED

The following weeks for Desi remained the same. Each day was filled with anxiety and fear. She was afraid of her father when she was at home, afraid of being violated at night, and at school there was the anguish of bullying. When she did find the courage to attend classes, she endured only humiliation.

Up until this point, though painful enough, the bullies merely tormented her with name-calling. Desi endured the usual routine of embarrassment in homeroom, appalling names shouted at her through the hall, and the fear of them being just around the corner. Lunch would finally arrive, where Desi usually had some relief by socializing with her new best friend, Jena. Desi never understood why Jena would even consider socializing with her. Things could have been much simpler for Jena if she never had been her friend at all. Perhaps it was in her nature to accept people for who they were.

On this day, they sat at the same table eating and talking as usual. Things seemed to be going well because for once when the bullies walked in they had nothing to say to her. Desi was puzzled.

After eating, Desi and Jena stood outside near the brick kindergarten building, talking about what the weekend had in store. From the corner of her eye, Desi spotted the bullies walking towards them. Their intentions seemed clear and fear took over.

"Hey, Fatso!" one shouted.

"We're talking to you, Dork," the other joined.

Desi froze, not knowing what to do or say. She'd never come face to face with them quite like this and she began to tremble.

"We're gonna kick your ass!"

Desi tried not to make eye contact. Maybe if she'd ignore them, they'd go away. Desi silently prayed.

Father, don't leave me now! Show me you're here! What do I do?

"*Trust me.*"

Startled, Desi wondered where the words came from but she continued to pray.

I've never been in a fight before in my life, except with Meagan, and then it wasn't a fistfight. Help me Lord. Please.

"*Trust me.*"

Desi tried to keep her thoughts in check while also trying to predict when the first punch would come. The girls closed in on her, and all of the students on the playground circled around to watch the fight. Some were chanting, "Fight, fight!" Others just watched and waited.

Desi stood there, unable to move. She wanted to run but she knew that they would catch her since she was too heavy to outrun them. She desperately wished to be at home in the safety of her room listening to music. Songs placed her in a different world; one without the pain and humiliation.

Just as the girls closed in on her, what could only have been a miracle had fallen into Desi's lap. The bell rang. Desi waited to see if the girls would ignore it and annihilate her anyway. The entire student body waited as well. They didn't want to miss a single moment.

As if someone or something told them to, they both retreated at the same time and went inside. Of course, as they walked away they announced that it wasn't over by a long shot and that next time she wouldn't be so lucky.

Desi breathed an enormous sigh of relief as if she'd been holding her breath the entire time. As she began to walk into the school, she silently thought, *Was that you God?*

Trust me.

Jena faithfully walked beside Desi until they had to part ways to their classes, neither of them speaking. All the while, only two words repeated in Desi's mind.

Trust me. Trust me.

Instead of going to her class, Desi retreated to the bathroom again as she always had when she couldn't face something. She sobbed and she wondered what she should do. As much as she hated it, she couldn't help but think that she needed to tell on the girls. In school, this tactic should only be used as a last resort. First, this would only make the girls hate her more. Secondly, who wants to be known as the tattletale? Especially in eighth grade! Junior High is supposed to be where you grow up, not immaturely rat on someone. Still, Desi felt as if she had no choice. It was either be a rat or get the crap beat out of her. In this light, she knew that telling was the only way.

Desi wiped her tears away and tried to wait for the redness to clear before heading to the principal's office. When she arrived, the secretary told her to have a seat while the principle finished her meeting. It seemed like a long time; however, she at least felt safe for the moment.

After a few minutes, the principle opened her door and invited Desi in. She was a warm, sophisticated lady with short blonde hair and every piece of clothing seemed to fit her perfectly. She wore a large diamond wedding ring and stunning white gold jewelry. Desi ached to be like her.

"So, what brings you to my office, Desi?"

Feeling at ease with her, tears began to stream down her face. She tried to take a moment to gather herself. When she finally spoke, it all came pouring out including every feeling, hurt, and heartache. She started at the beginning and ended with the close call on the playground. The principle just listened while trying to hold her emotions at bay.

When Desi was finished, the principle paused a moment and then reassured Desi that she will not have to worry about the girls anymore.

As much as Desi wanted to believe her, in the back of her mind she felt that it would never go away. She'd still have to go to the same school and see them every day.

Desi just half-heartedly smiled at her and said, "Okay."

"It seems that you've had a pretty rough day. Would you like to stay in the sick room until it's time to go home?" she asked.

Desi jumped at the chance. "Yes, please!"

The secretary led Desi to the sick room and suggested she might want to lie down on the couch. As she lay there, she felt partial relief. The sobbing had taken its toll and Desi drifted off to sleep. She dreamed of heaven and how there was no humiliation, no one was singled out, and everyone was beautiful.

*

The secretary nudged Desi trying to wake her up.

"Desi."

Desi slowly opened her eyes and when she realized where she was, she quickly sat up and fear took over.

"It's time to go home, Desi."

Home, Desi thought. *That sounds pretty good.*

"Thank you," Desi answered.

Desi gathered her things from her locker and headed towards the bus. On the bus ride home, Desi wondered what was going to happen to the bullies and what they

Cast Out Queen							K. Hohst

would do to her for telling on them. For now, she was safe. She would go home and isolate herself from the world and of course, listen to music.

TRUTH

When Desi entered the house, her sister was in the kitchen eating a typical healthy snack of fresh cut vegetables.

"Why weren't you on the bus, Meagan?" Desi asked as she reached for the Oreos.

"I got a ride with one of my friends. I can't wait until next year when I can drive."

"Yeah, then I won't have to ride that stupid bus!" Desi blurted.

"Maybe," Meagan answered.

"Where are Mom and Dad?" Desi asked.

"They're not home from work yet. Don't you have anything better to do than to bug me?"

Disgusted, Desi grabbed her cookies and milk then retreated to her room. She immediately turned on her radio and tried to tune in to a good song. Nothing seemed appealing so she went to her faithful collection of love songs and pressed repeat. She never seemed to get tired of these songs. They soothed and inspired her, as if it were therapy. Her stereo was the best gift she had ever received.

As she ate her cookies, Desi turned to the mirror and despised what she saw.

"Why do I eat this stuff?" she thought. "This is what's making me fat and yet I keep eating it!"

Depressed, she continued to eat until the bag was empty. She didn't know whether she felt nauseated because of the cookies or because she had another migraine.

Mostly her migraines arrived on Sundays. They would begin when she'd get home from church and last throughout the rest of the day. She would try to sleep it off because medicine never seemed to work. The other days of the week Desi suffered only regular headaches. There were only few days that she didn't have one at all. She was told that her vision played a part in her headaches and that she was supposed to wear glasses for this problem. Of course, Desi couldn't bear to wear them at school to avoid further remarks.

The headaches were only the tip of the ice berg when it came to Desi's health. She also suffered from chronic back pain. In fact, as a baby she didn't even walk until she had her first chiropractic adjustment. Her mother would tell her that she would just sit and never even attempt to crawl or walk. If that weren't enough, Desi had collapsed arches in both her feet and was told to get shoes that would give her the most support. Because of this and the fact that her feet were so wide, she often had to settle for shoes that weren't in style. Adding fuel to the fire, when she was four she had to get her tonsils removed. They were so enlarged she couldn't swallow her food. Prior to her surgery, Desi was thin as a rail but after she could eat properly so Desi began to put on weight. This, among other things, Desi dealt with day in and day out. Yet she always found a way to cope.

Desi's migraine was now worse and even the music wouldn't sooth her. She turned her stereo off and tried to find a comfortable position; on her side, of course. She finally settled with a pillow over her head and eventually drifted to sleep.

Later, Desi came out of her room for dinner and a shower then returned only to wallow in a pool of self-pity.

The following morning, Desi went to her mother's room and pretended that she was sick. She didn't want to face the consequences of tattling on the bullies. Besides, she needed to catch up on her homework. Staying home was beginning to be routine. Thankfully, her mother never questioned her motives and always let her stay home. Maybe it was because Desi's grades were always at least average or better, and she proved time and time again that she could be trusted to get her homework completed. Her mother, growing up Amish, wasn't required to finish school and so she never pressured Desi. Instead, she would just encourage her to do her best.

Meagan, however, always went to school. She fit in quite nicely at her new school and had an abundance of friends. One friend was Jennifer. She worked part-time for Meagan and Desi's parents at the restaurant they bought when they moved. Even though she was a grade older than Meagan, they'd still hang out together at times. They had study hall together in the library and the librarian made it quite easy for the students to socialize during this time.

Making small talk, Meagan asked, "Does your sister have any classes with Desi?"

She paused for a moment. "I hate to be the one to tell you, but my sister, Jill told me that Desi's really had a hard time in school.

There are these two girls that make her life a living hell. They call her every name in the book. Jill feels sorry for her."

Meagan was stunned but responded to Jennifer politely.

"Wow. I figured it wasn't great for her but I didn't know it was that bad."

"I'm sorry, Meagan."

"It's okay, Jennifer. Thanks for telling me the truth."

"You know," Jennifer added. "Not to brag, but my sister is popular at the Junior High and has lots of friends in her group. What if I would ask Jill to invite Desi to sit with them at lunch and maybe the bullies will lay off?"

"You would do that?" Meagan asked.

"Sure."

"Thanks!"

After Jennifer left the library, Meagan couldn't stop thinking about Desi. She felt horrible. She now realized why Desi was in her room so much and why she stayed home from school all the time. Meagan felt guilty for not seeing it sooner and not being a better sister. Though

Meagan knew Desi's troubles were not her fault, she still felt a responsibility to protect her.

Meagan was relieved when school was finally over. She wanted to rush home and talk to Desi. On the bus ride home, Meagan tried to concentrate on what to say to Desi. She wondered whether she should just come right out and tell her that she knew about the bullies. Desi could be very sensitive and Meagan didn't want to make things worse than they already were. She remembered how terrified Desi would look on the bus but never thought much more of it. She now knew where the terror was coming from. Meagan felt for her sister and wished she could make it all better.

Meagan walked into the house and immediately dropped her things to go find Desi. Of course, she was found in her room. Meagan tried to get a feel for Desi's mood.

"Are you feeling better?" Meagan began.

"Why do you care?" Desi snapped.

"I do care, Desi."

Desi was surprised that her sister didn't just snap back at her.

"Is there anything you want to talk about, Desi?" Meagan tried again.

"No," Desi lied.

Desi wanted badly to tell her sister, but she couldn't. Maybe, it was her way of controlling something in her life.

Besides, in her mind, Desi didn't figure that there was anything her sister could do to help.

Carefully, Meagan stated, "Jennifer told me a little of what's been going on with the bullies at your school."

Desi quickly focused on the floor, too ashamed to face her sister.

"I'm so sorry, Desi. Why didn't you tell me? You know I would have done something to help. Don't you?"

"There was no point in telling you, Meagan and there is nothing you can do."

Stretching the truth, Meagan stated, "Actually, Jennifer said her sister Jill wants to ask you to sit at her lunch table."

"You're just trying to make me feel better, Meagan."

"No, I'm not! I was talking to Jennifer in the library and she told me herself!"

Desi tried not to believe her. The mere thought of sitting at the popular table wasn't even possible to Desi.

Sitting with the popular girls, she thought. *There must be some mistake or Meagan is just lying. But why would she say that if it weren't true? She knows I'll find out sooner or later.*

"Desi," Meagan spoke. "Hello..."

Desi tried to focus on Meagan but still couldn't help but think about the hope of sitting with Jill and the popular group.

"What?" Desi replied.

"You were out in some other world for a minute. I was just checking to see if you were still with us."

"I'm fine. Just stunned is all." Desi answered.

"Hang in there, Desi. Things will get better. I promise."

"You shouldn't promise things you don't have control over, Meagan."

"I just have a really good feeling about this and that things will look up for you."

"Thanks, Meagan."

"No problem. And the next time there is something wrong, you had better tell me! Okay?"

"Okay," Desi smiled.

"Good. I'm going to go do my homework. Will you be alright?"

"I'm fine. Close the door when you leave though."

"Okay."

After Meagan left the room, Desi turned to her friend for help.

God, it's me Desi. Sorry to bother you but I just need someone to talk to. I'm scared. I'm scared of facing the bullies again and I'm scared of the possibility of sitting with Jill and her friends. What will I say? I don't even know what kinds of things they talk about. What if they talk about their boyfriends? I've never even had one. At least it's the weekend and I have two days before having to face it. I do appreciate that you've given me even a shred of hope. It is exciting and all but at the same time, the bullies might have a hay day with this. Give me strength to get through this year! I'm not sure how much more I can take!

Her mother knocked on the door.

"Hey Desi, are you up for dinner and a movie? Your father is going to stay at the motel across town this weekend to help start up the new restaurant."

"Yeah, I'm up for it!" Desi answered.

"Good! I'll go tell Meagan!"

When her mother walked away, Desi grabbed her jacket and rushed to the kitchen.

"I'll be out in the car, Mom!" Desi shouted.

"We'll be out in a minute, Desi." her mother answered.

She jumped into the front seat and anxiously waited. She remembered that she'd been in the middle of praying when her mother came to her room. Desi bowed her head and prayed, *Thank you Lord! Thank you! I have an entire weekend without worry or fear! Thank you! Thank you! Amen!*

Desi smiled while turning on the radio to find a good song, and for the first time in months, Desi felt at ease.

RESCUE

"Thanks for taking us to the movies, Mom," Desi graciously stated.

"Yeah, thanks Mom," Meagan added.

"You are very welcome, girls," she replied. "We need to do this more often."

After returning from the movies, Desi abandoned her usual routine of self-pity inside her room and opted to stay in the living room, laughing and talking. Each enjoyed their short time of freedom. Desi wished it would never end.

On Sunday, Desi and Meagan went to church with their Aunt. The cruel remarks targeted at Desi during Sunday school didn't sting as hard for once since she was mostly thinking about eating lunch with the popular girls. She did her best to ignore them and concentrated on what she would talk about at school.

During the sermon, Desi began to dwell on the bullies again. She tried to listen to the pastor, but with no success. By end of church, she had another migraine.

She was disappointed to spend the rest of the day lying in bed with the shades drawn. At least her mother would do her best to make her as comfortable as possible, which helped to ease Desi's disappointment.

Becoming routine, Desi turned onto her side as a fleeting thought of Jack brought temporary nausea to her stomach. She quickly thought of the hope her sister gave and soon she was asleep.

Monday morning arrived, and Desi tried her best to settle her nerves. Getting dressed, she silently spoke to God while also preparing for the worst. Desi chose a flattering pair of jeans and a pale pink sweater. After applying a bit of make-up to cover her acne, she wondered if it would be enough. Her stomach in knots, Desi couldn't even eat breakfast.

"Are you feeling alright, Desi?" her mother asked.

"I'm fine. I just don't feel like eating this morning."

Desi instantly knew she'd opened the door for her father to chime in. She waited for her Dad's insult to injury.

"Desi isn't going to eat? Well, that's a first!" he laughed.

No one was amused but did their best not to offend him. They were just grateful he was in a decent mood.

After breakfast, the girls gathered their things and headed down the driveway to wait for the bus.

"Hope everything goes well today, Desi." Meagan stated.

"Thanks."

She thought for a moment, and then looked at Meagan.

"I didn't tell you this before but last Thursday the bullies threatened to kick my butt at recess and everyone on the playground surrounded me just waiting to see it happen. Luckily, just before they annihilated me, the bell rang.

Afterwards, I found myself in the principal's office telling her everything that had happened since the beginning, which is why I didn't go to school on Friday. So even if Jill invites me to sit with them, the bullies are going to get me one way or another."

"Don't you worry about them, Desi," Meagan angrily announced. "I have friends older than them, and we'll make sure they don't ever touch you! Okay?"

"I'd love to believe you, but you don't know these girls. They have boyfriends that are in High School and I don't want to make things worse than they already are. We'll just see how it goes."

"Okay, but just say the word and I'll tell everyone I know!" Meagan assured.

"Thanks."

"By the way, who are these girls anyway?" Meagan asked.

"Jackie Thomas and Lisa Moore." Desi muttered.

"A Thomas girl?"

"You mean there are more of them?" Desi shook.

"Yeah, and they're all mean!"

"Great. How many are there?" Desi asked.

"Three that I know of…don't worry though. One has graduated already and the other hasn't seemed to bother my group of friends."

"That's comforting," Desi replied sarcastically.

"Seriously…Desi. Don't worry. Everything happens for a reason. You have to trust that."

"I really do try to remember that, but it's hard right now."

"I know, Desi. Just hang in there. Okay?"

"Okay."

The bus arrived and they both stepped on. Neither one was sure of what the day would hold for Desi.

Desi walked down the isle of the bus past the friendly face she'd grown accustomed to. She'd discovered his name was Scott and that he was popular with most everyone because of his wit and humor. He could make anyone laugh. For Desi, he made her both laugh and warm her heart. There was always a kind word for her. She sat in her assigned seat and tried not to stare.

When Desi walked into homeroom, the girls were already there and as Desi passed by, they quietly muttered a few choice obscenities so as not to get scolded from the teacher. Desi quickly sat down and didn't utter a word the remainder of the time. Jena didn't want to stir things up as well and followed Desi's lead. After homeroom, the bullies quickly caught up to Desi.

"Tattle tale!"

The other one joined in as well. Both the girls strolled along with Desi chastising her the entire way until they had to turn down another hall to get to their next class.

"Get out of my way, geek!" Jackie shouted while the other pushed her aside.

Shaking, Desi wondered how anyone could be so hateful.

Stunned, she stood frozen while they passed. She tried to pull herself together to face the next class.

"Three more hours before lunch," she thought. "Even if Jill doesn't invite me to their table, at least Jena will be there to make me feel better."

Desi walked into her first period classroom for Social Studies. While she didn't much care for the subject, she was at least partially comfortable in the fact that the teacher was pleasant and there weren't any students in the class that really took an interest in her, except of course for Scott. He sat in front of her and always did something that amused her. He was a straight A student, extremely intelligent, and never had to study. Despite his intelligence, he was what the students would call the "class clown" and did everything within his power to keep this title. Whether it was his comical remarks or merely a facial expression, it came easily and he was always the center of attention. Best of all, he always had a smile for Desi. Although it was never meant as a romantic gesture, it was still kind and sincere.

"Hey Des," he called to her.

Barely able to speak, she squeezed out, "Hi Scott."

His attention was quickly drawn to his real friends but Desi didn't mind. She loved that he called her Des, and this small amount of kindness was enough to melt away the humiliation in the hallway just minutes before. Desi felt warm and at ease just being close to him.

The rest of the morning went well. Lunch finally arrived, and Desi waited at the cafeteria door for Jena.

"Hey, Desi," Jena called.

"Am I glad to see you!" Desi announced.

"What's wrong?"

"I had a pretty rough morning."

"Oh."

Nothing more needed to be said. The girls proceeded to get their lunches and sit at their usual table, which consisted of several student types ranging from smart geeks, to just plain geeks. Some sat in solitude while others had a friend or two to socialize with. Desi and Jena usually chose the middle of the table to avoid the bullies. It rarely worked, since the bullies always sought Desi out regardless. So far, lunch was calm and the girls discussed what they would wear the next day. Then it happened.

"Desi!"

Desi was scared to turn around. She could tell it wasn't the bullies, yet she wasn't prepared to find out who was seeking her out this time."

"Desi!"

This time Desi couldn't ignore it. She glanced back to find Jill calling to her! Jill waved for her to come over, and Desi turned back to look for a reaction from Jena.

She told Jena to hold on and that she'd be back in a minute. Desi walked over to the girls, expecting to be laughed at or made fun of.

"Hey, Desi!" Jill started.

"Hey." Desi replied suspiciously.

Making conversation, Jill stated "My sister, Jenn told me that she is really good friends with your sister, Meagan. She also told me that Meagan says you're cool to hang out with. We were wondering if you'd like to sit with us at lunch."

"Sure! That'd be great!" Desi exclaimed.

"Great! Have a seat!" Jill encouraged.

Suddenly, Desi realized that she'd never thought far enough to imagine how this would affect Jena.

"What do I do?" Desi thought.

"Are you gonna sit down or what?" Jill asked.

Desi thought for a moment, and realized that she had no authority to speak on Jena's behalf and that popularity was the only way she would survive the rest of school without eventually getting it from the bullies. This was her only chance and as much as she hated to, she sat down without even looking back at Jena for fear of what she would see. Suddenly, a whole new world opened up for Desi. Jill introduced her to the rest of the group.

"This is Michelle, Sheila, Jessica, and Denise." Jill announced.

Intimidated, Desi answered "Hey."

"We were just talking about the upcoming dance next week and planning what we're going to wear and who we want to dance with!" Denise spoke.

Desi felt very welcome by most of the group; however, Sheila seemed unamused by Desi's presence. Desi tried her best not to let it bother her and focused on the rest of the girls.

"Who do you want to dance with, Desi?" Jill asked.

"I'm not sure, yet."

Desi knew right away whom she'd want to dance with, yet she wasn't quite ready to reveal her feelings for Scott and possibly face humiliation.

"Well, you have a month to decide and then prepare to ask if he doesn't."

"Okay," Desi agreed.

Though Desi considered the possibility of asking a boy to dance, she had no intention of ever going through with it. Still, she thought of the possibilities. She became so preoccupied with her new friends that she didn't even realize her lunch was still over at the other table.

Suddenly, the bullies were heading her way and fear broke out all over Desi's face.

"Why is *she* sitting with you, Jill?" Jackie shouted.

Jill just played it cool and politely stated, "Jennifer is friends with her sister and told us how great Desi is to hang out with."

"Whatever," the bullies muttered and then walked away.

"Thanks, Jill," Desi was grateful.

"Hey, what are friends for?"

Desi couldn't believe her ears and while the other girls weren't looking, Desi looked up and silently thanked God.

BLOSSOM

Since the rescue at the lunch table, things seemed to go better for Desi, despite here fears and insecurities at night. From the physical assault she'd endured, fear always gripped her at home but at least for the first time, she wasn't afraid to wake up and go to school. In fact, she felt a sense of excitement and thrill. It was a new experience that she never wanted to end. The bullies still made their presence known, but oddly the barrage of threats became fewer. Desi also now had more important things to focus on other than eating, and over the course of the next few weeks, she lost 15 pounds. If that weren't enough, a new treatment became available for her acne and Desi would be a prime candidate. The side effects were at times difficult, but Desi didn't seem to mind. In fact, many things she didn't seem to mind anymore. She now had bigger issues to concentrate on, the most important being the spring dance.

"Desi," her mother called.

"Yeah..."

"The phone is for you."

"I'll get it in my room!"

Desi darted to her room to find out who was calling. Butterflies jumped around in her stomach as she caught herself hoping it was Scott. When reality set in, she answered the phone.

"Desi, guess what?"

"Jill?" Desi asked.

"Yes! It's me! You'll never guess what happened."

"Does it have to do with a certain football player named Kyle?"

"Desi! He asked me to the dance! Isn't that awesome?"

"Calm down, Jill. You're gonna give yourself pimples!"

Jill laughed.

"You're so funny! Now, what should I wear to the dance, Desi?"

"I don't even know what *I'm* going to wear! My cousin lives just down the road from us, and she said I could go through her closet and see if there is something I want to wear. She has the coolest clothes!"

"I'm gonna have my mom take me shopping either tonight or tomorrow. Can you believe that I'm going to the dance with the most popular guy in school?"

Desi was happy for her new best friend but a part of her ached for the same feeling. Scott had been nice to her, but there was never a sign of anything more. Desi tried to focus on the fact that at least she was going to the dance and quickly pulled herself together.

"I'm truly happy for you, Jill."

"Thanks, Desi."

As if Jill could read her mind, she encouraged, "I'm sure someone will ask you to dance too. We'll make sure of that! Okay?"

"Okay."

"Desi!" her mother called.

"Yeah… Mom."

"It's time to go to Grandma's. Are you ready?"

"Hold on a second."

"I've gotta go, Jill. I'm going to my Grandma's house. My Mom and Dad are going out to eat with another couple, and Mom thinks we should go to Grandma's until they get back. Meagan's in High School for crying out loud!"

"Okay, I'll let you go then. See ya tomorrow at school."

"See ya when you get back from cloud nine!"

Jill giggled. "Bye."

"Bye."

*

"Hi, Grandma!" Desi opened the door.

Meagan greeted her as well and immediately found a spot on the couch to read.

Cast Out Queen   K. Hohst

The two of them were well trained. At Grandma's, there is nothing to do, and to go unprepared would be a big mistake. Having a conservative Amish family, there were many limits in which a person could have fun.

There was no television or radio and if you didn't like to read, as was Desi's case, your options were slim. Usually, the first thing Desi would do is raid the refrigerator, freezer and all cabinets. She would then end with the candy drawer. This time, Desi had no desire to eat. The only thing she could think about was the dance.

Desi plopped on the rocking chair and imagined what she'd be wearing and who would ask her to dance. Her eyes searched the quiet room. She stared at the empty chair where her Grandfather read every evening. The cup he spit his tobacco in was no longer there, and she wondered when it had been removed. Desi's Grandfather died of a heart attack a few months back, and though Desi was sure her Grandma was mourning him, she never let on as she sat quilting. As long as anyone could remember, there was always a quilt set up in the middle of the living room floor and it was a thrill to watch it progress. It began by taking up the entire room and as she worked, she would roll up the end that was finished until there were only the last few inches remaining. Sometimes people would pay her to quilt their blankets and other times, she would piece together her own from leftover scraps. Everyone admired her patience and skill.

Desi's grandmother had snow-white hair and wore the traditional Amish uniform, which was the bonnet, a plain dress held together with pins, and black stockings. At a family reunion one year, the grandmothers were all sitting together in a line. All the cousins determined that Desi and Meagan's Grandmother was the cutest of them all. Her shy and mousy stature along with her height of barely five feet tall made it an easy decision of who was the cutest.

She always seemed so humble and for Desi, she would always be the tiny Amish woman holding a special place in her heart.

The clock struck eight, and Desi wondered how she would last the rest of the evening without the television. She began to daydream about the dance again and tried to picture her and her new friends on the dance floor. Then it dawned on her.

I don't even know how to dance! Desi panicked.

"Meagan! I need your help!"

"I'm reading my book. Go away."

"You have to help me now! The dance is this weekend and I don't know how to dance!"

Meagan sighed and stared at Desi for a long time. Finally, she agreed and motioned Desi to follow her upstairs so she could show her without bothering Grandma. Desi tried not to act too relieved but couldn't quite contain her excitement.

As she headed up, she remembered all the times they slid down those stairs on pillows. She chuckled to herself and wondered what in the world they were thinking.

Desi and Meagan went into one of the three bedrooms, moved a few things out of the way, and then began.

"Okay." Meagan started. "This is going to be a breeze. First you need to figure out what your beat is.

I'll start the beat by clapping and you follow the beat by snapping. Once you get the beat, I want you to shuffle your feet back and forth with the beat. Like this."

Desi watched in anticipation. Thinking that it didn't look so difficult, she followed her lead.

"Yes! That's it! That's the basics of it. And if you want to get some variety, you can turn and start the same beat, or you can switch off between clapping and snapping. It just depends on the song. And try to shake your hips if you can. You know, show some sex appeal. Do you get it?"

"Yeah, actually I do!"

"You're really good, Desi and I'm not just saying that. You have good rhythm and learn fast!"

It was unusual to be complimented by her sister or anyone else for that matter. The only thing that Desi ever succeeded in was singing. Once, Desi was lead in a musical play at church, and she shined. She could hit any note, and her personality fit the part perfectly. During a practice, one of the boys in the older youth group asked Desi where she learned to sing like that. Desi tried not to show it but inside she was beaming with pride.

Desi continued practicing long after Meagan had gone back downstairs to her book. She danced in front of the mirror and suddenly stopped. She took a good long look at herself and couldn't believe what she saw. Her hair had grown longer and was accented with a spiral perm. Her face had cleared up considerably from the treatment, her body was taking shape, and for once she wasn't disgusted by what she saw.

Knowing that she would never be a model or something glamorous like that, she was still pleased. She remembered what her oldest cousin had said to her once.

"One of these days you are going to blossom and when you do, you will appreciate it and be that much more beautiful for having it inside as well."

Desi repeated that phrase in her head until she finally believed it. She had blossomed and it was a feeling that she'd never experienced before. She only hoped that it would be enough.

I am enough.

Desi listened.

I am enough, my child.

Desi was relieved to hear His voice again and realized she hadn't heard it in some time.

Since that day on the playground when the bullies threatened me? she thought. *Surely not that long.* Taking in this new information, Desi was faced with the fact

Cast Out Queen						K. Hohst

that since everything had been going well, she'd forgotten about the One who'd always been there for her. God.

THE DANCE

After searching in her cousin's closet for an outfit, Desi finally managed to find the perfect look. She chose a soft pale blue sweater with a V-neck and buttons down the front. She decided to wear the sweater with the V in the back and then accent it with pearls. They then paired the sweater with a jean miniskirt to capture a dressy yet casual look.

"It's perfect, Desi," her cousin encouraged.

"Thanks."

"I knew we'd find something for you to wear."

Desi glowed with pride. "Because of you…"

Desi changed back into her other clothes and thanked her again for the outfit.

"Well, I'd better get back over to the house or Mom will be wondering why it's taking so long. I'll let you know how the dance goes, okay?"

"Good luck, Desi."

*

Desi was just putting the finishing touches on her make up when Meagan knocked on her door.

"Can I come in Desi?"

"The door is open," she answered.

Meagan was surprised when she saw Desi. "Wow! You look great!"

"Thanks."

"Are you nervous?"

"A little," Desi lied.

Again, Desi covered up the truth. The fact was that Desi couldn't have been more terrified. *Would anyone ask me to dance or will I end up in a corner somewhere while all the others dance with the guys?*

Meagan could see that she was trembling. "It's going to be fun, Desi."

"I hope so."

Desi looked at herself one more time in the mirror and decided there was nothing more that she could add to her appearance.

Meagan picking up on Desi's elation hesitantly stated, "This is the first time I've seen you this happy since before you spent the night with Skyler."

Desi instantly tensed.

"It's been difficult for me, Meagan."

"I know it has because you haven't been the same since."

"You have no idea what I went through that night"

"What are you not telling me, Desi?"

Desi's hands began to sweat and her breathing became harsh. She looked down at her fumbling hands as she tried to muster the words she'd been holding in for so long.

"Jack didn't just ask me to get in bed with me. When I woke up I was lying on my back with my legs spread open and underwear pulled down. He was…"

Desi couldn't say the words. Now that she was older, she knew what it was and how to describe it but she just couldn't say it out loud.

"What is it, Desi? Tell me. You can tell me anything. I'm your sister."

Desi tried again. "He…"

Again, the words failed her. Her breathing was ragged and she turned her back to Meagan.

"Tell me, Desi. Please."

Desi took a deep breath, and released her deep dark secret. "He was eating me out…licking my privates."

Stunned, Meagan was speechless as her mouth dropped open.

Desi looked down in disgust and waited for Meagan's response. Oddly enough, as she waited, she began to feel relief. It was as if a fifty-pound weight had been lifted from her shoulders and she felt light as a feather. As the weight lifted, she felt a joy that she'd not known in a long time. Just as she began to smile, Meagan finally spoke.

"I'm so sorry, Desi. That must have been horrifying! Why didn't you tell me?"

"I didn't know what it was and at the time couldn't have possibly described it. You saw how long it took me to tell you even now. I can't sleep on my back anymore because that is how I woke up. I'm afraid every night that I go to bed. It's like a disease that can't be cured. Although, since I've told you I seem to feel like it's not as scary anymore. Something happened when I finally told you the truth. It somehow minimized the fear. Maybe it's because I'm no longer alone in it."

"Oh, Desi... What can I do to help?"

"You've already helped. By convincing me to tell you, I feel like the healing can begin now. Thank you"

"Are you going to tell Mom," Meagan asked.

"No way!" Desi emphatically shouted.

"Do you want me to tell her for you? She has to know."

"I don't care. Do what you want but I'm not telling her."

"Okay, I will do it." Megan assured.

"Thanks."

"No problem, Sis. I hate that I didn't know all this time and you were alone in it. That bastard needs to pay for what he did."

"It's okay, Meagan. I'll be alright. You don't need to protect me."

"We will see what Mom says about it."

"Whatever," Desi mumbled. "Right now, I don't want to think about it anymore. I just want to go to the dance and forget it ever happened for now."

"Okay. Let's go."

"Start the car and I'll be right there." Desi stalled.

After Meagan left the room, Desi seized the opportunity to say a short prayer.

Father, I have to make this fast, but I just wanted to thank you for helping me tell Meagan about that night. I feel a lot better now. Also, could you please be with me tonight and help me to not make a fool out of myself? Protect me from any harm and may the dance be a success. Thanks! Amen.

*

Desi cautiously entered the school. Even though the bullies hadn't harassed her as much, Desi never stopped watching or waiting for them to be just around the corner. This was also the first activity outside of school she had attended and didn't know if they would be there. Desi approached the cafeteria where she spotted her group of friends. She started to make her way towards them but before she could get there, she noticed Jena. She was sitting alone and appeared to be nervous and miserable. Desi tried to think of what to do.

Jena looked towards Desi's direction, which made the situation worse. Desi briefly smiled at Jena and waved. Jena humbly waved at Desi and then looked away as if she knew Desi wouldn't be coming over to her. Relieved, Desi walked towards Jill and the others.

Jill noticed Desi walking towards them. "Desi, is that you? You look fab! Great outfit!"

Everyone else joined in and complimented Desi. Everyone that is, except Sheila. For no apparent reason, she didn't like Desi from the start and nothing she could do seemed to satisfy her. For now, Desi would just have to act as if she didn't notice or take an approach that her mother taught her, kill them with kindness.

"Has anyone danced yet?" Desi asked.

The girls all looked at each other and without any other response, Desi could tell they hadn't and were terrified to do so. Desi looked around the dance floor to see if anyone else had dared to test the waters. Desi noticed quite a few people dancing, but no one of high status. Desi had been at the school long enough to know who was in and who was out. She took a moment to listen to the song that was playing and determined that it was a good beat to start with. Feeling at ease, she turned to the others and found herself in new territory. It seemed her new friends either didn't know how to dance or were too scared to go out there. It was apparent that if they were to have any fun at all, Desi would have to make the first move.

"Are you guys ready to dance or what?" Desi playfully asked.

Again, they all looked at each other for approval and then back at Desi. Finally, Desi grabbed Jill's hand and headed out on the dance floor. The rest followed as well. Desi found the rhythm immediately and soon realized that the others didn't know how to dance.

Desi stopped and proceeded to tell the girls exactly what Meagan had taught her. The girls seemed pleased with the results and they all began to loosen up and enjoy themselves. Even Sheila was having a good time and began to lower her defenses with Desi. Perhaps, she thought that Desi hadn't much to offer but now that she had taught them to dance, she realized that she did have something to give in return for their sympathy. Desi didn't seem to mind and was relieved more than anything.

As Desi turned, she caught a glimpse of Scott entering the cafeteria. Desi's legs became weak and her heart was beating wildly. Desi watched as he crossed the room to his friends. He briefly caught Desi's eyes and before she could find out what he would do, she quickly looked away.

She thought, *what is your deal, Des? He may have waved or even joined us on the dance floor! Next time, I'll have the courage to say something.*

Cast Out Queen   K. Hohst

The girls remained dancing until finally a slow song began. They immediately took their places alongside the wall and waited for the guys to make their move. Desi looked for Scott but didn't see him. Kyle asked Jill to dance first.

Where is he? Desi thought. Soon, all her friends were dancing until only she was left standing. Desi was humiliated.

This is great, she thought. *How embarrassing.*

As if that weren't enough, she noticed that Scott asked someone else to dance and she had to stand watching the whole thing on the sidelines. Desi could feel her cheeks become hot as tears pricked at her eyes. After, what felt like an hour, the song was over and as her friends approached her. Desi couldn't hold it in any longer. She covered her face to hide the humiliation. Desi wanted to run to the bathroom, but she didn't want her new friends to be offended.

The girls didn't know what to do to help, and so they tried to encourage her as much as they knew how. Denise told her, "Just wait until the guys get to know you like we do." Jessica added, "Yeah, once they get to know you, everyone will be asking you to dance." Jill's comment seemed to comfort Desi the most. "Look at me Desi," she instructed. "You are a great person, and if they can't stop long enough to see you on the inside, then they aren't worth your time anyway."

Desi could feel the warmth from her friends and tried to let them know they were helping. Only, there was a slight pain in her heart as she thought further about Jill's comment. The reality was that Scott did take the time to acknowledge Desi and for the most part, he was slowly getting to know her. The painful truth was that he still wasn't interested. Desi would have to prove herself and this was going to take more time than she would like. Still, she felt the dance was a partial success and for that she was grateful. She cleared up her eyes and headed out on the dance floor with the rest of them.

Desi noticed that Jena was dancing with some other girls and though Desi still felt sick to her stomach over what she had done, she was glad that Jena at least looked as if she were having a good time.

Maybe someday, she thought, *I'll have the guts to talk to her and apologize.* For now, she would squeeze as much fun out of the evening as she could, before having to leave and face whatever circumstances her home life would bring.

FREEDOM

After the dance, it was arranged that Jill's mother would take Desi home. The ride home was short since she only lived just a mile outside of town. The two laughed and talked about the memorable evening. When they pulled into the driveway, Desi graciously thanked Jill's mother for the ride.

"I'll call you when I get home, Desi."

"Okay. Talk to you in a bit! Thanks, again!"

Desi watched as they pulled away from the driveway and it was only then that she heard the yelling. Without even thinking, she knew it was her parents and as usual, most of the yelling was coming from her father. Desi began to tremble as she wondered what had set him off this time.

Did Meagan tell Mom and Dad what I said? Why would they be fighting about that? What should I do? Desi agonized. Desi's heart began to beat faster. *Should I go inside?*

She decided to walk behind the house to see which room they were in. She couldn't see them as she looked through the sliding glass doors, which meant that they were in their bedroom. She silently entered the back door, hoping that her father wouldn't hear her come in. Desperately, she tiptoed down the hall past her parent's room and ever so slightly turned the doorknob to her sister's room. Slowly, Desi peeked through the opening of the door.

"What is going on?" Desi whispered.

"Quick!" Meagan urgently commanded. "Get in here before he hears you!"

Desi did as she was told. "Did you tell Mom already?"

"No I didn't and I don't know what started it," Meagan voice shook."

"Has it been long?"

"No. It just started right before you came home."

Suddenly, they heard their mother scream and then shout for someone to call the police.

"What's wrong with Mom's voice?" Desi asked.

"It sounds like he's choking her!" Meagan trembled as she picked up the phone.

Suddenly, she paused.

"Dial it, Meagan." Desi anxiously pushed.

Meagan couldn't move.

Desi desperately tried again. "Dial it!" *Why isn't she calling?* Desi thought.

Meagan knew she would have to eventually answer to her father and she didn't want to find out how he would react, even with the sound of her mother's screams ringing in her ears.

Desi couldn't take it anymore and ran to her room. It was farther away from her parent's room and she wouldn't have to hear as much.

Desi agonized as she covered her head with her pillow to drown out the sound. *God, help us! Please don't let him hurt her!*

Without warning, he dragged their mother out of the room and down the hallway to the living room. He called for Meagan and Desi to come as well. This was something entirely different than usual, and had no idea of what to expect. Until now, they'd been spared a firsthand look at their fights.

Desi quickly found a place on the floor and Meagan sat on the couch near her mother.

"Do you know what your Mother has done to me?"

Desi was so terrified that she had to wrap her arms around her waist so that her father wouldn't see her shake. She didn't know what was to come and figured this could be the night that he would turn his aggression on them. Desi tried not to stare, but she could see that her father's eyes didn't look right. They were glazed over as if he were someone else. It was like an alcoholic rage but without the alcohol.

Her father shouted it again. "Do you know what your Mother has done to me?"

Desi looked at her mother and saw the same terror that Desi was feeling. Desi wanted to run and hug her.

"Your Mother has refused me!"

Meagan and Desi looked at each other for just a moment as if to say, "Is he for real?" Their attention was immediately turned back to their father as he continued shouting and belittling their mother.

Then he declared, "Now, I've worked hard for a lot of years to get this house and all the things in it." He turned his attention to their mother.

"If you want to throw it all away, then that's just fine. You can leave. I'm going to the kitchen to get a drink and when I get back, I want you to answer me. Are you going or are you staying?"

When he left the room, Meagan and Desi watched their mother as she whispered to them, "What do I do?"

I want her to be able to leave, God, but don't let her go without me! Please! I don't want to stay here with him!

Neither of the girls knew what to say and in a matter of seconds, he was back.

"Well, what are you going to do?"

She tried to steady her voice as she spoke, "I think it would be better if I left."

No one was prepared for what his reaction would be. He immediately became more hostile than before and each soon realized that their mother had chosen the wrong thing to say.

"I am not losing everything because of you!" He picked up the wooden stand that was sitting in front of him and slammed it back onto the floor as each one jumped from fear.

Terrified, tears began prick at Desi's eyes. She could no longer hold in her fear.

Their mother was desperate to stop this insanity and before she could think, she blurted, "I'll stay! I'll stay!"

Instantly, it was as if it were a switch, he calmed. He demanded the girls to go to bed as their mother followed him to their bedroom.

Desi lay there wondering what had just happened and desperately tried to make sense of the whole thing. She couldn't hear anything coming from their room but the thought lingered, *"Did he make her do it?"* The thought was too much to bear and she immediately tried to think of something else…anything else. She resorted to what worked in the past.

Heavenly Father, be with each one of us. Thank you for the blessings that I recognize as well as the ones I do not. Forgive me for my sins and let me start a new day tomorrow. Protect Mom and comfort her tonight. Give her courage to get through this night and help her to decide what is best. Oh Lord, don't leave me here with him alone but set Mom free from Dad.

Trust me.

Desi was glad to hear the soothing voice again. With the stress of the evening and the hour nearing 4:30 a.m., Desi's fears began to fade as fatigue set in. For now, she would have to trust that God had a greater purpose and eventually things would be okay.

Cast Out Queen K. Hohst

*

Over the following months, Desi's mother did leave and went to live with her mother just down the road. Desi and Meagan were left behind to live with their father, while their mother figured out a way to get them with her. She struggled to resist his every trick and deceit. He tried it all, everything from guilt, threats, and even religion. The religion phase was hardest on the girls because he would keep them up at all hours of the night reading the Bible to them, even on school nights. It was a scary and ugly place for Desi, yet she was happy that her mother was protected.

On Mother's Day weekend, Desi and Meagan were missing their mother and decided that whatever it would take, they would find a way to be with her.

Meagan took on the role of telling their father that they were going to stay with their mother for a few days for Mother's Day. At the same time, Desi snuck out the back door with everything that she could carry to the car. After several trips, the car was full.

They went out the front door with a small packed bag and told their father they'd be back in a few days, each of them knowing that they would never look back.

Of course, he was furious when he'd realized what had happened. Oddly, he didn't confront Meagan or Desi. Instead, he turned his rage towards their mother. When she was close to giving in to his threats, Meagan took her stand.

"You are not going back! He will hurt you worse next time. He can't hurt us anymore. You are free! Do you understand? You're free!"

Her mother listened as Meagan's words slowly sank in.

Desi could see that Meagan had gotten through to her and from that moment on she pressed forward with divorce proceedings. It was a spiteful divorce solely from her Father's side and if not for the judge, her Mother would have ended up with nothing. She did obtain some of the furniture and it was enough to start over in her own place. Luckily, the restaurant was in her name, and she could keep it in order to make a living. There were times when he would show up and try to talk sense into either the girls or their Mother, but for the most part, he would get nowhere and eventually gave up.

Meagan graduated High School and was given the opportunity to move in with one of her friends from school. As for Desi, she stayed with her Mother and worked for her at the restaurant. Her sophomore year had just begun, and she'd just gotten her driver's license. She began to really enjoy her freedom, and for the first time in her life, there was no fear. Desi even began lying on her back for moments at a time to face the anxieties that plagued her at night. Meagan had finally told their mother about what had happened but to Desi's relief, nothing was spoken of it.

SLAVE DAY

Ironically, Sheila and Desi became very close friends after that night at the eighth-grade spring dance. Since Desi had gotten her license, she would pick up Sheila every morning for school. They settled into a routine of stopping by the Quickie Mart for a candy bar and a soda, then off to school. One day, it was very foggy and Desi had borrowed a car from one of the employees at her mom's restaurant because her car was in the shop. They pulled out of the Quickie Mart and headed down the three-mile stretch that led to the High School.

"What is this woman's problem in front of us? We're going to be late if I don't pass her!"

"Be careful, Desi." Sheila warned.

"I don't see anything coming. I'm going for it. Hold on!"

Sheila gripped the door handle.

"Here we go!" Desi shouted as she put the car into fifth gear.

She was just alongside of the car when she realized that there was another car with only one headlight coming right towards them!

"Desi!" Sheila shouted.

With only a split second to react, Desi had to make the decision to either continue passing or back track. She floored the accelerator and before she even knew whether she'd cleared the car she was passing, then swerved over into the right lane to safety.

"That was so freakin' close!" Sheila shouted. Do you know how close you came to hitting both cars?"

"I have no idea! With the fog and shear panic, all I could do is react!"

"It had to be just inches in either direction!"

"Man! That had to be a miracle or something!"

"Someone upstairs must like us." Sheila agreed.

Desi added, "Thank the Lord I had this car because mine would never have made it!"

Desi silently thanked God as they pulled into the driveway.

Both girls shook as they walked towards the school.

"Hey girls!"

Desi and Sheila turned around to see who was calling them. Desi began to tremble even more.

"Hey Scott."

"What's wrong?"

They told him the whole story as they walked to their lockers. All the while Desi was trying to decide whether her heart was pounding more from the close call or that Scott was near. Even after all this time, Desi's heart beat wildly just thinking about him. As they finished telling Scott the rest of the story, Desi noticed that he was listening intently and not at all amused. He looked worried, in fact. Desi soon brushed it off and figured he was just not in a good mood.

The close call was the talk of the school. The day went quickly due to shortened classes for the school assembly. Every year the juniors and seniors could purchase the freshman and sophomores in an auction traditionally called Slave Day. Upper classman, would pay to have the under classman as a slave for one whole school day. And almost anything goes.

Everyone anxiously filed into the gymnasium to see who would be the next to endure slave day.

The freshman and sophomores were put into various groups to be displayed for auction. Luckily, Desi was placed with her group of friends and when it was their turn, Desi anxiously waited to see who would bid on them. It was soon apparent that two groups wanted to buy them. One group was their siblings and the other were the boyfriends. Jill's Sister Jennifer also participated with Megan. Since they were graduates, Meagan and her friends had appointed one of the seniors to bid for them.

I hope Meagan's group wins the bidding. I feel so stupid because I don't even have a boyfriend and they probably don't even want me. They are just bidding to get their girlfriends. How humiliating.

Trust me, daughter.

Desi was soothed, yet still felt humiliated.

Cast Out Queen	K. Hohst

The bidding had reached $300.00 and had broken a record for the most amount raised in the auction since the tradition began. The final bid was $350.00 and Desi had gotten her wish. Meagan and her friends won the battle. Desi felt relief but soon she would face a different kind of humiliation.

*

The next day, Desi and Sheila walked into the school not knowing what to expect. They were to report to the bathroom where Meagan, Jennifer and her friends would reveal what they had planned. Given the amount of money spent, Desi was sure it would be unpleasant. When they arrived at the bathroom there was complete chaos and hysteria.

What is going on in here?" Desi exclaimed.

"Our sisters!" Jill shouted.

Desi began to giggle when she discovered that all five of her friends were wearing wrestling outfits with Ultra Mega gel in their hair standing straight up, and old 45 phonograph records hanging on each of their ears.

"You look ridiculous!" Sheila added.

Desi laughed.

"Yeah, laugh some more! You're next!" Jill snapped.

Meagan jumped right in, "Here Desi. Get dressed!"

"You realize that you'll pay for this, right?"

"Yeah, we already paid $350.00! Now get dressed!"

Sheila and Desi reluctantly did as they were told and when they were all finished, Meagan gave them each a few more accessories and sent them on their way. That is, except Desi.

"Wait." Meagan said. "I almost forgot! Put these on!"

Desi was mortified when she realized that she would have to walk around the entire day with scuba diving flippers!

"You've got to be kidding! I can't walk in those!"

"Yes, you can and you will!" Meagan scolded.

Desi put them on and just as she started out the bathroom Meagan added one last thing to complete her creation. In addition to an already grueling costume, she'd also have to carry around large cast iron frying pan.

"Thanks, Meagan. You're the best." Desi remarked sarcastically.

"Have a great day!" Meagan and Jennifer shouted.

Desi could hear them laugh as they exited the building.

Unbelievable! I knew it would be bad but this is a little much.

By this time, the bell had already rung and the halls were empty. As if this weren't bad enough, she had to walk past the library where there was a sizable homeroom in session.

Of course, everyone had full view of the hallway through the large windows that lined the wall. Carrying her frying pan and her books, Desi tried to walk as fast as she could but with little success. Just as she was halfway past the library, one of Desi's flippers got caught in the register of the floor. Desi and the frying pan flew into the air and landed with a bang! Desi was so horrified that she didn't even notice if the students in the library were laughing at her. She picked up her things and rushed as quickly as she could to her first class. When she finally made it, she immediately searched out Sheila for comfort.

"Sheila! You will never guess what happened! My flipper got caught in the register right in front of the library and I fell in the hallway so freakin' hard that I bent the frying pan!"

Sheila could only laugh. "That is hysterical, Desi! If it were going to happen to anyone, it would be you!"

"Thanks for the support, Sheila."

The rest of the day everyone and anyone teased Desi. Whether it was about her fall or her ridiculous flippers, it didn't matter. Desi already had a reputation of doing crazy things.

She'd tried out for volleyball and after three days of conditioning, Desi was so sore that she could hardly move.

Cast Out Queen K. Hohst

This made it increasing difficult to arrive at her classes on time. One class she couldn't afford to be late because when you weren't at your seat when the bell rang, a detention was imminent. So of course, Desi ran into the classroom screaming in writhing pain, "My legs! My legs! My legs!"

The teacher laughed so hard that Desi became the first to be late and escape his class without a detention.

Then there was the time in physical education when everyone had to demonstrate an exercise. Of course, Desi waltzed up in front of the entire class and displayed what she called her forefinger exercise. It simply consisted of moving the forefinger up and down. Again, the class and the teacher were so amused that she got away with it. There was also the lunchroom episode that students and teachers alike never let Desi forget. Basically, Desi was drinking her milk when someone made her laugh and milk shot out of her nose.

With today's incidents, Desi was sure to clench the title of "Class Clown."

Desi finally made it through the day and as she walked towards her car dressed in her normal clothing again, Scott called for her to wait for him.

"Hey, Scott."

"Hey darlin'."

Oh, my gosh! Did he just call me darlin'? Desi could hardly think straight but she regained her composure and made small talk.

"Did you have a good laugh at my expense today?"

"Yep, I sure did!" he teased.

"Thank you very much, friend."

"Well, if it helps, you look great now!"

Desi did her best to stay calm and kindly answered, "Thanks Scott."

"You betcha! See you on Monday!"

"Later, Scott!"

Desi remained calm until she reached the car.

Oh, my gosh! Oh, my gosh! Oh, my gosh! Did Scott just say that I looked great or was that my imagination! Thank you, Jesus! Thank you, Jesus!

I'm always with you, daughter.

Again, Desi thanked him from her heart.

Thank you, Lord.

Cast Out Queen   K. Hohst

SLEEP OVER

Scott and Desi had become close friends over the past couple of years but Desi never let him know that she had feelings for him. She didn't want to risk their friendship. They were now seniors and the end of the year was nearing. Desi was anticipating the prom coming up but was disappointed that she hadn't been asked yet. She'd had just one or two possible leads on a boyfriend throughout High School, but nothing serious ever evolved. She would hold out for Scott even if it meant no boyfriend at all.

The end of Friday finally arrived and she was looking forward to another fun weekend with the girls. She walked to her car and waited for the opportunity to get out of her parking spot. While the other cars around her were leaving, she noticed Jena sitting on the bench by herself waiting for a ride. Desi had never mustered the courage to make things right with her since that day she was asked to sit with the popular group. It had been a slow process but Desi was making progress with her confidence and insecurity issues. She could feel a tugging to go over to her and apologize but the mere thought made Desi squeamish.

I can't do it, God. I'm too embarrassed. She'll never forgive me!

Go, daughter.

Desi tried to ignore the voice and started to drive away.

Go.

Desi tried to fight it but reluctantly found a new parking space and turned the engine off.

You need to help me, God. I'm no good at this.

There was a silence. Desi soon realized that she'd gotten herself into the mess, and she'd have to get herself out of it.

Her entire body trembling, Desi got out of the car and walked towards Jena. Butterflies began to rumble in her stomach as if it were the first day of school.

As Desi approached, the two girls scarcely made eye contact before Jena quickly turned away.

Desi took a deep breath and whispered, "Help me, God."

"Hey, Jena." she began.

Jena turned to Desi with a look of bewilderment and returned the gesture. "Hey."

"Can we talk?" Desi asked.

"Sure. I guess."

Desi couldn't read her expression and wondered what she'd gotten herself into.

"I just wanted to apologize for my behavior that day in the lunch room when we were in Middle School. I honestly didn't know what to do. I didn't have the guts to ask on your behalf, and I couldn't turn them down because I was sure it was the only chance I had of making it through the year without getting creamed. Is there any chance that you can ever forgive me?"

Jena's expression was unchanged, and Desi was sure that she'd made an even bigger mistake.

Desi was about to turn away when Jena warmly smiled at Desi and spoke with the softest and kindest voice she'd ever heard. "There is nothing to forgive. I may have even done the same thing. Although, I might have apologized a bit sooner." Jena teased.

Relief washed over Desi realizing she'd done the right thing.

"Jena, you are the most amazing person I've ever known and I'm truly unworthy of your friendship. I was wondering if we could start again where we'd left off. I can introduce you to the rest of the girls. But know this. Whatever their reaction, you will be my best friend. I'll never let anything change that again."

Completely moved by Desi's words, tears began to surface in Jena's eyes.

"I'd like that."

"Actually, I'm supposed to go to a sleep over at Sheila's house tonight and they will all be there. This would be a great opportunity to join the group. I'll call Sheila and explain and then I'll call you and let you know what she says. If I know her well enough, she'd be glad to have you. If not, you'll come to my house tonight, okay?"

"Are you sure you want to do that?" Jena asked.

"Never been so sure of anything in my life!"

"Okay, then."

The girls exchanged phone numbers, and Desi walked away feeling better than she had in a long time.

"Faithful daughter."

Desi looked up and smiled, knowing she'd done the right thing, and guilt would no longer grip her.

*

As soon as Desi had gotten home, she immediately picked up the phone to call Sheila and although she was nervous, she couldn't help but get excited. She felt as though she were bursting at the seams while she waited for someone to answer.

"Hello." Sheila finally picked up.

"Hey! It's me, Desi."

"Hey, there!"

"You will not believe what just happened!"

"Slow down, Desi. What's up?"

Desi told her the story from the beginning and left out no details. When she'd finished, she anxiously awaited Sheila's response.

"That took a lot of guts, Desi."

"You have no idea!" Desi giggled. "So, what do you think? Would it be alright if Jena comes tonight?"

"Well, I know I was a jerk to you when you first joined our group and I'd like to think I've learned from it. I think it's a great idea, Desi."

"You don't know what that means to me, Sheila. I think you'll really like her."

"It's settled then. Everyone is coming around 6:00. See ya then?"

"Yep. See ya!"

"Hey, Sheila."

"Yeah?"

"Thanks."

"Any time. Bye, Desi."

"Bye."

Without delay, Desi called Jena to let her know. The two decided that Desi would pick her up at 5:45.

Desi arrived right on time. Jena motioned to Desi to wait a minute while she said goodbye to her mom and dad. As Desi waited she noticed how much Jena's appearance had changed. Her blonde hair had now grown below her shoulders and she'd also gotten contacts. She didn't wear any make up, but she didn't need it because of her flawless skin. Desi wondered if Jena was taller than her or if it was the fact she was so slender that it made her seem taller. Jena was stunningly beautiful.

Jena walked towards the car with her things and Desi jumped out of the car to help her.

"Let me help you," Desi offered.

"Thanks. I hope I didn't bring too much."

"Not at all! You wouldn't believe the things we haul to these sleepovers!"

Both giggled and hopped into the car.

"This is going to be a blast!" Desi announced. She was clearly trying to sooth any anxiety Jena could possibly have.

The girls arrived just after 6:00 and all the other girls had already arrived. Desi and Jena looked at each other briefly and then got out of the car. They headed towards the door with their things and Sheila came rushing out to greet them.

"Hey! You girls look overloaded! Need some help?"

"Thanks. That would be great!" Desi answered.

When they'd gotten everything inside, Sheila turned her attention to Jena.

"So, you must be Jena! I've been looking forward to meeting you ever since Desi called. I've seen you in school but I've never actually had a conversation with you. Don't we have the same lunch?"

"Yeah, we do. Thanks for letting me come with Desi. That was really nice of you."

"Well, let me just say that if you are even half as fun as Desi is, we're going to get along great! Are you hungry? The rest of the girls are in the kitchen pigging out on pizza and ice cream."

"Sounds good to me!" Desi agreed. "What do you think, Jena?"

"That would be great!"

"Come on!" Sheila motioned. "We'll introduce you to the other girls."

"Jena and Desi are here!" Sheila announced.

Everyone turned in their direction and for a moment, Jena wasn't sure what their reaction would be but soon everyone was saying hello. Desi and Jena joined in the food fest and before long everyone was giggling and doing their best to make Jena feel welcome. Desi was confident that once Jena felt more comfortable, her wit and charm would surface and the girls would just love her.

The rest of the evening consisted of movies, makeovers and phone calls to boys. Desi was right. It didn't take long for Jena to relax, and she soon had fit right in with the group. Finally, at about 4:00 in the morning, everyone settled into their sleeping bags. Desi and Jena were next to each other, which gave them a chance to chat before falling asleep.

"I can't believe I'm still up, Jena. I have to work with my Dad in the morning. He called me last week and asked if I would meet him to help with a job he is doing for someone's patio. It's two hours north of here. I don't know if I was brain dead at the time, but I said yes."

"I heard that your Mom and Dad had gotten divorced. I'm sorry."

"Believe it or not, it was the best thing that ever happened to us. I've never known freedom like I have had in the last couple years.

He's okay to be around, now that he doesn't have control over us. He always tries to win us over with money or eating out in expensive restaurants. Now that we don't see him as often and don't see the ugly side of him, I can tell he really does try the best he can. I've been told that because he was the oldest of the family, his father was really mean to him. That helps me to understand his temper and the violence he has never been able to control."

"That's good that you are able to keep in contact."

"Yeah, I guess. I always dread it, but then it ends up better than I thought it would. Anyway, I probably should get some sleep."

"Yeah, you should. Before you go to sleep though, I just wanted to tell you what a great time I had tonight. It was a blast!"

"I'm so glad! God works things out in the strangest ways."

"I'm learning that!" Jena whispered.

"See ya in the morning." Desi yawned.

ACCIDENT

Desi dropped off Jena after leaving Sheila's house. They'd planned to go shopping together on Sunday to buy prom dresses. Jena already had a date, which stung a little for Desi, but she was truly happy for her and was looking forward to the shopping spree.

The two-hour drive wasn't as bad as Desi had imagined. Playing her favorite songs made it bearable. For Desi, there was nothing better than a great song. She enjoyed a variety of music, although a ballad was still her favorite. Whether Pop, Country, or Rock. It didn't matter. The song would take her to a place that she could only dream.

Desi finally arrived, and she was pleased that she'd followed the directions correctly the first time. Her dad was already there and unloading the materials from his truck.

"Hey, Dad." Desi's hands trembled.

She was nervous working for her father because he was a very impatient person and quite the perfectionist. She knew he'd try his best, but sometimes his best would end in yelling.

"Desi!" he answered. "You made it!"

"Yep! And on time too!"

"I see that! Well, let's get started so you can get home before it gets dark."

"Okay. Do you want me to help unload?"

"Sure. Take these."

He handed her some tools and led the way to the back porch. They would be installing an enclosure for the porch and he proceeded to explain to Desi what they'd be doing. He'd already been there the day before putting up the walls and so they began to install the first of the windows.

"Alright, Desi. Hold on to this end while I put in the screws."

"Okay."

Desi held the window as he struggled to make the window fit.

"Hmm." He said.

"What is it, Dad?"

"It doesn't fit for some reason. Let's put the window back down and I'll do some measuring."

He got his tape measure out and did some figuring. Desi was always amazed at her father's skill. He could do anything. He was a carpenter, a farmer, taught himself blueprinting, was a truck driver, could work on cars, got his pilot's license, his Real Estate license, and could sell swampland to someone if he needed to. Desi remembered how late he'd stay up at night just working on numbers. That was his specialty. He could do math in his head and rarely used a calculator. She recalled when he'd gone to school to get his Real Estate license and ended up teaching the class! Those were the moments when she could brag about her Dad. Desi smiled as she looked on at him.

"Well, you won't believe what I did, Desi. I didn't measure the windows right. I'm going to have to reorder them."

Desi was shocked that her dad was so calm. Relaxed even! Even more so, Desi was amazed that he'd messed up. She couldn't recall a time that he'd made any mistake when it came to his work.

"Well, let me go tell the owner that we'll have to come back in a few days to finish."

"Okay."

Awesome! Desi thought. *Now I can go home and sleep! This is too good to be true! God, was that you? Of course, it was. Duh. You control everything.*

Her dad returned. "Well, Desi. You came all the way up here for nothing."

"That's okay, Dad. Sorry, that you had to go tell the owner you messed up. Was he upset?"

"No. He was nice about it."

"That's good. Do you need me to come up again?"

"Well, I'll need to install them in the middle of the week and you have school so don't worry about it. I'll manage."

"You sure?" Desi asked.

"Yeah, it's fine."

"Okay then. I'm going to go."

"Here some money for your trouble. He handed her a fifty and Desi graciously took it. She wasn't at all surprised and in fact, she half expected him to.

"Thanks, Dad. That will help with my prom dress!"

"Prom, huh?" he answered.

"Yep. It's a month from now."

"Well, have fun!"

"I will! See ya, Dad!"

"Bye, Desi."

Desi got into her car and strapped in. She waved goodbye as she left and couldn't help but wonder how she got off so easy. She searched the radio for a good station and headed home. She decided she'd stay awake better with some of her favorite songs playing. Desi reached behind her to grab the case of music. It wasn't budging and she looked back for just a second to see what the problem was. Suddenly, she could feel that she had gone off of the road into some gravel and when she realized what she'd done, she turned back and tried pull the passenger side tires back up on the road. The gravel was too loose and it just kept dragging her more off of the side of the road.

Desi couldn't fight it any longer and headed down the steep ditch. The ditch was flooded and the car forced the water up on all sides. She couldn't see a thing. Desi panicked and just held tight to the steering wheel, unaware if she'd even tried using the brakes. All at once, the car came to a halt and Desi was forced forward into the steering wheel.

She didn't know if she'd blacked out but someone was opening her door and asking if she was okay. Desi's head hurt and she couldn't see clearly enough to make out the stranger's face.

"Are you okay, sweetie?" he spoke again.

Desi's mouth felt pasty as she tried to form the words. "I don't know."

"Someone call 911!" he shouted. She hit a telephone pole and she's bleeding.

Desi could hear in the background someone saying medics were on their way. She was relieved to hear this but wondered how long it would be as the pain began to really set in. Desi tried to move.

"Stay where you are, honey. You might have a neck injury."

Desi did as she was told and began to feel sleepy. She hoped it was only because she'd stayed up too late the night before but instinctively she knew it wasn't. She closed her eyes but the stranger's voice spoke again.

"Stay awake, honey. Please."

He sounded so kind, Desi thought.

She could hear the sirens and was immediately fearful of how painful it might be when they load her into the ambulance.

Desi went unconscious and when she woke up she was in a hospital bed with her mother sitting next to her.

"Oh, thank God you're awake, Desi!"

Desi's head was pounding and she ached all over. "Am I alright, Mom?"

"The doctor says that you hit your head pretty hard and that you have a concussion. You will be alright in a few weeks though."

Desi was relieved and relaxed her muscles a bit. "How bad do I look?"

"Well, let me show you!" She pulled a compact from her purse and placed it in front of Desi.

Desi freaked. "Mom! I look horrible!"

Her eyes were black and blue and her lips were twice their normal size. She had a bruise on her forehead and she could see some cuts on her neck where the seat belt had etched against her.

"Desi. The doctors said you would heal quickly and it would hardly be noticeable by prom."

"Thanks, Mom." Desi could always count on her mother to know just what she'd need to hear.

"Guess what?" her mother smiled.

"What?"

She looked at her watch. "There is someone here to see you that has been in the waiting room for five hours now and I'm sure he'd love to talk to you."

He? Desi thought. "Who is it?"

"I think he said his name was Scott."

Desi's eyes shot wide open. "Scott is here? Are you sure he said Scott?"

"I'm fairly certain. Also, your whole group of friends are here and so I'll tell them all they can come see you now."

"Mom, can you put some powder on my face, please?"

"Sure." She applied the make up as careful as she could without Desi climbing through the ceiling and then went out to get her friends.

I can't believe he came! I look a mess! I'm sure he's expecting it but it might be more than what he's prepared for. Why did he come? Why would he wait that long? Calm down, Desi. He's a good friend and he's just worried about me. Chill out.

Desi waited anxiously for them to come. She noticed her Bible lying on the table beside her. Her mother must've brought it. Desi smiled and closed her eyes. *Thank you, God for protecting me. I know how easily you could have taken me if you'd wanted to. Although I look forward to seeing you someday, I'm glad it wasn't today. Obviously, you have work for me to do and so I'll keep my eyes and ears open. Again, thanks. Most of all, thanks for bringing Scott here. Amen.*

Desi could hear a crowd of people approaching. She stiffened. The door slowly opened and she saw Jena first.

"Hey, Desi."

Everyone joined in and gathered around her bed. Scott stood behind the girls like a true gentleman.

"Hi guys. Thanks for coming."

Everyone chatted for a few moments, and then Sheila asked, "What happened, Desi?"

Desi did her best to explain what had happened as each one held on to her every word.

"The doctors said that you were lucky the water in the ditch slowed the car down enough before you hit the telephone pole." Jena stated.

Desi could feel that the pain was increasing and asked if someone would get the nurse. Jena volunteered and the others realized that Desi was too uncomfortable to visit any longer.

"Well, we'll let you get some rest, Desi. You're probably tired." Sheila stated.

"Thanks for coming guys. It means a lot to me."

Desi put pressure on her temples to ease the pain. Scott came to her side and caressed her hair.

Everyone said their goodbyes and left the room. That is, except for Scott. Desi's heart began to beat wildly as she realized they were alone.

"I'm really glad you're okay, Desi. You had me really scared. I've been praying for you most of the time you were unconscious."

Desi was pleasantly surprised that he'd prayed for her or even prayed at all for that matter. She knew he went to church but wasn't sure of his relationship with Christ.

"I'm sorry. I didn't mean to worry you. I must look awful right now."

"You've never looked more beautiful to me, Desi."

Am I imagining this, God? Does he really think I'm beautiful? Does he have feelings for me, too?

"Thanks, Scott. You always know how to make me feel better."

Jena came back with the nurse and she administered a pain reliever through her IV. After the nurse left, Jena noticed that everyone left except for Scott. She immediately realized that she was a third wheel and decided to give them time alone.

"Your mom said you could come home on Wednesday. Do you want me to come over to help you settle in?" Jena asked.

"That would be great. I'll call you when I get home."

"Okay. I'll call you tomorrow to see how you're doing."

"Thanks, Jena."

"Anytime. Bye Scott.

"Bye Desi."

Jena closed the door behind her and Desi turned to Scott.

"Desi. I've been thinking about us a lot lately. Especially since your close call a few weeks ago with Sheila.

Desi realized that Scott had been worried when she'd told him about the foggy day. Her insides smiled.

"I'd planned to do this sooner but I was afraid of your reaction. But now I realize that life is too short and I'm not going to waste another minute of it."

"I've liked you since tenth grade. I was just too nervous to ask you out. With uncertainty, he put her hand in his."

Tears pricked at Desi's eyes as she felt the warmth in his hand and the sincerity in his voice.

"Will you go to the prom with me? Not just as my date but as my girlfriend."

Desi couldn't hold the tears in any longer and she reached to pull him closer.

"I've never wanted anything more. I'm not dreaming, am I?" Desi asked playfully.

"This is as real as it gets."

He moved closer and softly kissed her on the lips. Desi couldn't even feel the pain. All she could feel was the passion and the heat of his touch. Her insides tingled as he pulled away.

"I love you, Desi. I always have."

"I love you too, Scott."

REDEMPTION

Scott stayed with Desi the remainder of her hospital stay, except for the occasional times he would go home to shower. Desi's mother didn't allow him to sleep in the same room but she was very impressed by his loyalty and was quite taken with her daughter's new boyfriend. Jena visited the hospital every day and when Desi returned home, she stayed with her at Desi's house while she finished recovering.

After a few weeks, Desi was finally given clearance to leave the house, however she wasn't allowed to drive. Jena didn't have her own car so she drove Desi's car and took her to the mall to get a prom dress. They searched several stores and hadn't found just the right dress.

"Let's try this store, Desi." Jena suggested.

"Okay."

As soon as they walked in, Desi's eyes focused immediately on a dress hanging on the wall. It was a full-length black dress with shimmering pink trim and sleek black mesh draped across the shoulders. That's the one! Jena. That's the one! I love it!"

"It's gorgeous, Desi. Let's see if they have your size! What is your size anyway?"

"I'm not sure. I lost some weight while I was in the hospital. Let's try a size eight."

"Great! Right here is one! Go try in on, Desi."

"I'm so excited I can hardly stand it! Will you come with me?"

"Sure! Let's go!"

The girls went into the dressing room and Desi quickly put on the dress. It was absolutely striking on her. The dress was just the right length and it complimented her every feature.

"This is the one, Jena. I love it! Will you look at the tag to see how much it is?"

Desi closed her eyes and prayed it wouldn't be too expensive.

Jena was cautious, "It's $199.00."

"Wow! I have enough and with the money my Dad gave me, I can get shoes and accessories!"

"Awesome! Let's go get it then!"

"Right on!"

After purchasing the dress, the girls spent the remainder of the day getting accessories, planning their hairstyles and eating junk food in the mall. When they returned home, Scott had left a message. He was checking on her to see how she was feeling. Desi still hadn't quite gotten used to having a boyfriend, much less Scott. Her eyes lit up just at the sound of his name.

"I'm going to go take a shower if that's okay, Desi. That will give you a chance to call Scott back."

"Thanks, Jena."

Desi dialed the number Scott had left for her and waited for someone to answer.

Butterflies would inevitably creep in her stomach each time she would call; yet as soon as she'd hear his voice, they calmed instantly.

"Hello." A voice answered.

"Is this Jimmy?"

"Yep. Sure is."

"This is Desi. Is Scott there? He left a message for me to call him."

"Hey, Desi! Hang on and I'll go get him."

Desi could here Jimmy call for him and she anxiously awaited his soothing voice.

"Hey there, sweetie."

"Hey, Scott."

"How was the shopping spree?"

"It was a blast! I got the perfect dress. Do you want to know what colors you'll be wearing?"

"Hmm. I don't know if I do or not." He teased.

"Well, here it is anyway. It's a long black slender sexy dress with shimmering pink trim."

"Let me get this straight. I'm going to be wearing pink and black?"

"Yep. And you'll like it." Desi laughed.

"You know what?" Scott asked.

"What?"

"You're right. I will like it. Because you are going to look gorgeous and I can't wait to see you in it!"

"Well, two more days and then you can."

"I don't know if I can wait that long!"

Desi giggled. "Sure, you can! What choice do you have?"

"Well, I could come over right now and have you try it on."

"No way! It's a surprise. I'll tell you what though. You can still come over!" Desi taunted.

"I suppose, it's better than nothing. I'll be over in about an hour. We have to finish our video game first."

"That's fine. That will give me a chance to shower. See you then?"

"Yep. See ya soon. Love you, Des."

Desi loved when he called her that.

"Love you too."

*

Prom night finally arrived and Desi's day was carefully planned so that she'd be ready at 7:00 p.m. sharp.

Jena, Sheila and Desi all had tanning appointments at 12:00 p.m., nail appointments at 2:00p.m., and hair appointments at 4:00p.m. They would break for lunch, snack in-between appointments, and be home at 6:00p.m. to get dressed and put on finishing touches.

The girls had a blast and eagerly anticipated their long awaited Senior Prom.

Desi was ready by 6:45, which was perfect so she could spend some much-needed time in her Bible. She went to her favorite. The book of Job. Desi could often relate to the suffering of Job. Just the mere fact that he experienced such despair and agony, yet never wavered in his faith. He would cry out to God in his pain but still could recall God's promises of redemption. One verse stood out to Desi and it was found in Job chapter 5, verse 9.

Desi turned to this passage and read. *He performs wonders that cannot be fathomed, miracles that cannot be counted.* She clung to this hope in her many years of sorrow and misery. When she felt alone and discouraged, she found strength in just this one passage. As she read it again, she smiled.

She heard the doorbell ring and she could hear her mother greeting Scott.

"Desi!" her mother called.

"Coming!"

She closed her Bible and placed it on the nightstand. She took one last look in the mirror and was satisfied with the outcome. She opened the door to her bedroom to find that Scott was waiting for her just outside the door.

"You are absolutely stunning, Des."

Desi gazed at how handsome he looked in his tuxedo. His blonde hair was perfectly gelled and it was more apparent in a tuxedo, that he lifted weights. Desi was utterly captivated.

"Thank you. You don't look so bad yourself." Desi giggled.

He leaned in closer and kissed her softly on the lips. Desi's heart began to beat wildly and as he pulled away, he gently took her hand and led her to the entranceway where her mother waited to take pictures. Scott carefully pinned on the corsage he'd brought, which matched perfectly. They took a few photos and then he led her to his car. As usual, he didn't miss an opportunity to be a gentleman as he opened the door for her and helped her in.

"So, where are we going to eat? I'm starving!" Desi asked.

"It's a surprise."

"You've been saying that all week. Can't you tell me now?"

"Nope."

"Fine. Have it your way then."

"Good. It's better this way."

They drove towards the city and Desi anxiously waited for what he had in store. When they finally arrived, she still couldn't make out where they were going because there were no restaurants that she could see. Scott parked the car and helped Desi out. He placed his arm around her waist and led her down the block around the corner. There, waiting for them was a horse drawn carriage and one red rose lying on the seat. Tears swelled in Desi's eyes as she realized the trouble he'd gone to for her.

Without hesitation, she hugged and kissed him on the cheek.

They rode a few blocks before arriving at a restaurant that sat on the river. They were escorted to a table with a perfect view of the city along the water.

Breathless, Desi tried to speak. "You don't have to do all this to impress me you know."

"I know what you are about, Desi and what you stand for. That's why I want to treat you like a Queen. From what I've gathered, you haven't had too much of that in your life and I want to be the first to do it. Is that alright with you?"

"Yes, Scott. It's wonderful."

They had dinner and rode the carriage back to the car so they could go make their appearance at the prom.

When they arrived, Desi immediately watched for her friend, Jena.

"Do you see Jena yet?"

"No. Not yet. We'll look for her when we get inside. Are you cold? I can put my jacket around you."

"I'm fine. Thank you, though."

Scott gently wrapped his arm around her and led them inside. The music was loud and most everyone was dancing. They entered the ballroom area and Scott spotted Jena.

"There she is, Desi. Want to go say hello?"

"You read my mind! Let's go!"

Desi anxiously grabbed Scott's hand and they made their way over to Jena.

"Jena!"

"Desi! You're finally here! What took you so long?"

"Well, we took a carriage ride."

Jena was impressed, "Wow! That's awesome!"

"I know! Is this your boyfriend, Jeff?"

"Yep. That's him!"

"Hi, Jeff. I'm Desi and this is Scott."

"Hey. Nice to meet you both."

"How did you two meet?" Scott asked.

Jena replied, "He's a freshman in college, and he has an internship with my Dad networking computers."

"Cool." Scott responded. "You look great, Jena." he added.

"Thanks!" Jena blushed.

A slow song began, and Scott politely declared, "Well, that's my cue. I've been waiting all night to dance with my Desi, and so if you'll excuse us, we'll catch up to you later, alright?"

"Sounds good to me." Jeff replied. He turned to Jena. "Shall we?"

"I'd love to!"

Scott and Desi made their way to the middle of the dance floor. He wrapped his arms around her waist and moved in closer. Desi placed her arms around his neck and searched his eyes.

She wondered how it was possible that she was on the dance floor with the kindest and most considerate person she'd ever met. Her wonder and amazement was short lived when the verse in Job came back to her. *He performs wonders that cannot be fathomed, miracles that cannot be counted.*

"What are you thinking, Des?"

"I'm thinking that this could very well be the most wonderful night of my life."

"Well, I know that it's my most wonderful night."

Desi beamed with delight as she rested her head on his shoulder. He carefully caressed her long locks of hair and kissed her neck softly. They pressed against each other and Desi's insides ached. She knew that she would have to take extra care to not get into a situation that she couldn't get out of. Scott made his intentions clear on one of their

Cast Out Queen   K. Hohst

recent dates that he was saving himself for marriage. Desi was in complete agreement with him and that made him all the more attractive to her. Even so, they would need to be very careful. Desi was forthcoming with Scott about what had happened at her neighbor's house. She found that each time she spoke of it, there was further healing. As if, it was therapy. Scott was sympathetic and was careful to make her feel safe with him. Desi respected him for that.

The song ended and Desi tried her best to control her emotions. They pulled away and moved towards the remembrance table. There, they made conversation with several friends and studied the enormous collage that the Student Counsel had created. Both laughed at some of the pictures of when they were freshman and how much they'd changed.

They then shifted directions to the lobby and had their picture taken together. There was a stand next to the table where each person was to vote for the King and Queen of the prom. Desi had no trouble at all with her decisions. She voted Scott for King and Jena for Queen.

One of Desi's favorite songs began and she asked Scott if it would be okay for her to dance with her friends. Scott encouraged her to go, and said he'd go get them some drinks.

Desi gathered her friends and headed for the dance floor. Desi cherished each moment of the song, knowing that this would probably be the last time they'd all be together in a setting like this. After the song was over, each one hugged and wished each other well in whatever the future held. Desi's emotions got the best of her and she was sure that her makeup was smudged. She went to the restroom to freshen up before meeting Scott.

She then headed to the lobby and as she approached him, Scott walked towards her with a glass of punch. They decided to go find a table and rest for a few minutes. They chose a table not far from the D. J. and sat down.

"So, how was the dance with the girls?"

"Emotional, to say the least."

"You women."

She smiled. "God gave us these emotions for some reason I guess."

"I suppose."

The music stopped and the D. J. began to make announcements. He began with announcing that someone had left their lights on in the parking lot. Everyone had a good laugh. Next, it was time to reveal who had won the title of King and Queen. Desi had struck up conversation with another classmate sitting near them and wasn't at all paying attention. Suddenly, Scott was tugging at Desi to get up.

Bewildered, Desi asked, "What is it?"

"You're the Prom Queen, hon. They want you to go up to the front!"

Just then they announced that Scott was voted King.

Cast Out Queen   K. Hohst

Desi was motionless. She couldn't understand how she would be voted Queen. Scott softly took her hand and escorted her up to the front. They placed a crown on her head and presented her with a dozen roses. They placed the King's crown on Scott and began playing "*I could not ask for more.*"

They motioned for Scott and Desi to take their place on the dance floor as they announced the King and Queen of the prom. Scott gently held her close as he caressed the back of her neck, and Desi embraced him warmly.

The reality of the evening's events began to take shape. There she was on the dance floor with her first love and named Prom Queen. The song was equally fitting. She recalled the first day of school when they'd just moved there and what she'd endured. She was a complete outcast, and there seemed to be no hope.

She marveled at how a situation could at one point seem so desperate and then to another become so extraordinary. As the moment sank in, Desi closed her eyes and from the depth of her soul, thanked her Heavenly Father for what was most certainly a perfectly orchestrated miracle.

Author's Notes

The story of my childhood did in fact include an abusive home life, molestation, bullying, and God as my companion. My sister did rescue me by orchestrating a new group of friends and my parents did get a divorce. These two events changed everything. If you're wondering, I was voted prom queen my senior year. I reiterate these facts for one purpose. If God could do this in my life, imagine the possibilities in yours!

The result may not be the same as mine, but God promises in Romans 8:28, "...in all things God works for the good of those who love him, who have been called according to his purpose." (NIV) Take comfort in knowing that God's promises cannot be broken. If you are going through something difficult, please do not give up! The best years of my life came after the age of 27! I met my husband, had three children, and have four grandchildren. I finished my first book at age 45! I thought that nothing could surpass being prom queen. I was so wrong.

Imagine if I'd given up during the rough times. I would have missed out on so much. Honestly, I would have given up if it weren't for my Savior Jesus Christ. Without Him there is no hope at all. Please do not misunderstand me. Life was not perfect after being prom queen. My health has always been a challenge. When I was 40, I was diagnosed with Multiple Sclerosis. I experience pain in some way nearly every day. We are not promised a perfect life, but we are promised that He is always with us.

Everything in this world is temporary and a test for what is to come. We all have a choice. The choice to include Jesus in our life is the only one that really matters. If you have not asked Christ into your life, please take the necessary steps to do so.

If you have never been exposed to the Good News of Jesus, let me share it with you. In Genesis, we read that God created Adam and Eve to oversee His new creation. Incredibly, He gave them free will. This means we have choices. (Never accuse God of allowing bad things. He gave us free will and there are people who abuse this freedom.)

Satan then comes into the picture to mess everything up. He temps Eve into eating the forbidden fruit and Adam did as well. This allowed them to see good and evil. Because they disobeyed the one and only rule given to them, God put a curse on mankind. From that moment, sin was now something that had to be atoned for. In other words, we must pay for our sin.

Initially, the sin had to be paid for in an animal sacrifice. (I know that sounds harsh but once you study the scriptures, you will come to understand this) Animal sacrifice was a temporary atonement until the timing was right for a Savior to come and take our place by dying for ALL sin.

Here is where reality of this incredible story takes shape. **There was a man named Jesus documented in Roman history. He is not a made-up character**. He was accused of calling himself God and found guilty. He was crucified on the cross and placed in a tomb. On the third day, the incredibly large and heavy stone was rolled away from His tomb.

Here is where it gets interesting. Jesus had a massive following during the three years He preached to others about the Good News. When He was crucified, their hopes and dreams of a king to save them was destroyed. However, when the tomb was found empty, many of His followers witnessed Him alive. **For forty days, Jesus appeared to countless people. The rising up of His following became even stronger than before. What other theory can explain the sudden shift Christ's followers?** The belief of this following was so strong that many died sharing the Good News to others. Their desire was for everyone to know Jesus and even though the Romans persecuted them, they never backed down or recanted their beliefs.

The Romans tried to explain away the empty tomb by claiming His body was stolen. If Jesus were still dead, how did the massive uprising come to be? **During the trial, crucifixion, and His death, most of the followers scattered, denied knowing Him, and went into hiding. Again, why the sudden shift? It was because Jesus was alive.**

After the forty days, Jesus ascended into heaven; however, in His absence He provided the Holy Spirit to anyone who would ask for forgiveness, believe in the crucifixion/resurrection, and ask Him into their life.

Once you truly realize your need for Christ and the Holy Spirit fills your life, your eyes are opened and you will see things that you never had before. It's truly as if you are blind and then after putting on a pair of glasses, you can now see! **No words can describe an encounter with God**. I had a relationship with God during my adolescence; however, I didn't experience the Holy Spirit until I was 24. That is when the cobwebs were removed from my eyes and I began to see as God does.

After all these years, I am still learning and growing. It is a lifetime walk with Christ to achieve even a fraction of what He can do through us.

I've only shared the basics of Christianity with you. There is so much more I would like to share, but it would take up at least another book to cover it. If you believe you are ready to ask Jesus into your heart, I've given you a prayer at the end to do so.

If, however, you need further information, I would recommend several things. First, there is a website called gotquestions.org that has a vast amount of information in an easy to read format. Secondly, reading the Bible is crucial. Reading it from cover to cover is difficult but beneficial. You can also read the New Testament first, which may be easier to absorb initially. Regardless of your method, scripture is God-breathed and is vital for growth. Rushing through it just to get it finished is not recommended. Before reading, ask God to open your eyes to truths that have been hidden from you.

When I was in college, I decided to put in writing the questions and answers that an individual needed in order to understand the need for Christ. I will share this with you. When you realize your true need for Christ, pray the prayer at the end. Please know that you are not required to change first before asking Him into your heart. Once you take that step of faith, He is the one who empowers change. Believe me, I know.

SALVATION

Where do we find the answers to salvation?

II Timothy 3:15: "And how from infancy you have known the Holy <u>Scriptures, which are able to make you wise for salvation</u> through faith in Christ Jesus."

Why do we need salvation?

Romans 5:8-9: "But God demonstrates His own love for us in this: while we were still sinners, Christ died for us. Since we have now been justified by His blood, how much more shall we be saved from <u>God's wrath</u> through Him!"

Romans 6:23: "For <u>the wages of sin is death. But the free gift of God is eternal life</u> in Christ Jesus our Lord."

How do we receive salvation?

John 3:16: "For God so loved the world that He gave His only begotten Son, that <u>whosoever believes in Him</u> shall not perish, but have eternal life."

John 14:6: "<u>Jesus</u> said to him, "<u>I am the way, the truth and the life. No one comes to the Father, but through me.</u>"

Why do we need to repent?

Luke 13:3: "I tell you no! But unless you repent, <u>you too will all perish.</u>"
Luke 13:5: "I tell you no! But unless you repent, <u>you too will all perish.</u>"
II Peter 3:9: "The Lord is not slow about His promise, as some count slowness, but is patient towards you, <u>not wishing for anyone to perish,</u> but for all to come to repentance."

How do we repent?

Acts 3:19: "Repent, then, and <u>turn to God</u>, so that your sins may be wiped out, that times of refreshing may come from the Lord."

Why is it so important that we do not hesitate for a moment to receive salvation?

Matt 24:4: "So you also must be ready, because the <u>Son of Man will come at an hour when you do not expect him.</u>"

I'm ready to receive Christ. How do I do this?

Heavenly Father, I want to start a relationship with you. I admit that I am a sinner and that I can only be made clean through your Son Jesus. I repent by turning away from my sin. I realize that I alone cannot overcome sin without your help. I believe Jesus died for my sins and rose again, which now enables me to be holy and to be in your presence for eternity. I accept this gift and ask Jesus to come into my life as my Savior. I invite the Holy Spirit to fill me and guide my life. Amen.

If you've prayed this prayer, we are now family and you are forever in God's Kingdom! Your name is in the Book of Life! Revelations 20:15 reads, "And if anyone's name was not found written in the book of life, he was thrown into the lake of fire."

Now that you are a believer, I would recommend dialogue with your new friend in Christ. Talk to Him about anything! He knows your heart so there is no need to hide anything. Invite Him in to each day and call on Him frequently. You will be amazed at how He aides you throughout the day. I was in accounting a good portion of my work career and I discovered that when I couldn't solve a problem, I would ask Him to help me and without fail, He did! I highly recommend this practice. It serves to strengthen your faith.

If you've received Christ or would like to comment on something, please e-mail me at wwjdgal1@gmail.com. God, bless you on your journey!

May everyone come to know God's love...

www.ingramcontent.com/pod-product-compliance
Lightning Source LLC
Chambersburg PA
CBHW071514040426
42444CB00008B/1641